LIES THAT CHELSEA HANDLER TOLD ME

OTHER BOOKS STARRING
CHELSEA HANDLER

Chelsea Chelsea Bang Bang

LIES THAT CHELSEA HANDLER TOLD ME

BY CHELSEA'S FAMILY, FRIENDS AND OTHER VICTIMS

INTRODUCTION BY CHELSEA HANDLER

A CHELSEA HANDLER BOOK | BORDERLINE AMAZING® PUBLISHING

GC

GRAND CENTRAL
PUBLISHING

NEW YORK   BOSTON

A Chelsea Handler Book/Borderline Amazing® Publishing

Hachette Book Group
237 Park Avenue
New York, NY 10017
www.HachetteBookGroup.com

Printed in the United States of America

Originally published in hardcover by Grand Central Publishing.

First Trade Edition: April 2012
10 9 8 7 6 5 4 3 2 1

A Chelsea Handler Book/Borderline Amazing® Publishing is an imprint of Grand Central Publishing. Grand Central Publishing is a division of Hachette Book Group, Inc.

The Grand Central Publishing name and logo is a trademark of Hachette Book Group, Inc.

The Hachette Speakers Bureau provides a wide range of authors for speaking events. To find out more, go to www.hachettespeakersbureau.com or call (866) 376-6591.

The publisher is not responsible for websites (or their content) that are not owned by the publisher.

ISBN 978-0-446-58470-8 (pbk.)

Library of Congress Control Number: 2011921993

This book is dedicated to Michael Broussard. He is responsible for every book I've written, and for every bridge I've burned in the book world. I love you dearly, you great big homosexual. Stay gay. It gets better.

Contents

Contents

Introduction

My name is Chelsea Handler and I'm not proud of myself. I have made a career out of being a misanthrope with the maturity level of an eight-year-old who had to repeat the third grade several times. Am I pleased with myself? Sort of, but I am *definitely* not proud. I know that I should be more mature than I am, and I have sometimes tried to curb my behavior, but it never seems to take. I have to come to terms with what it is I have to offer the world, and obviously what it is isn't mind-blowing.

So, in the vein of giving back to the community, I have figured out a way to give back to a handful of the people I harass on a regular basis. Everyone who contributed to this pile of nonsense is someone who is very dear to me, and someone who needed cash. I believe in spreading the wealth. Give, give, give, and laugh, laugh, laugh. Even when it's at the expense of others, it's important to laugh. Laugh loudly, laugh often, and most important, laugh at yourself.

For those of you who have read my other books, the names of some of the recurring characters in this book may confuse you. The reason being, when I first started writing books, I was instructed to change all names and likenesses to protect people and their privacy, and also to protect myself from being sued by people I had allowed to penetrate me.

However, it turns out that everyone in my life has somehow warmed up to the idea of being humiliated in print, and are now adamant about my using their real names going forward. Here's a key:

Sidney = Simone
Sloane = Shana
Greg = Glen
Ray = Roy

There are more, but I've already lost interest in explaining this and would prefer for everyone to get to the part of the book that will, I hope, hold your interest the longest.

In closing, I would like to thank each and every one of you for making me a *New York Times* bestselling author. It is a sad testament to the state of this country, but I will take what I can get, when I can get it, and try to laugh at the fact that it happened at all.

xo,
Chelsea

LIES THAT CHELSEA HANDLER TOLD ME

Chapter One

Zookeeper

JOHNNY KANSAS

C helsea Handler is a menace. Working for her is very much like working for a highly functioning, over-sexed, drunken chimpanzee. Just when you think you're part of the family and it's all fun and games, she turns on you and bites off your fingers, nose, and genitals.

As with any volatile primate, you can never tell when

Chelsea and me in Anguilla last Christmas.

1

she'll attack, but through years of experience and close observation I have concluded that she is most dangerous when she's bored or has a little free time and is looking to entertain herself. Now I understand why they put toys in monkey cages. You want to keep them busy so they have no time for mischief. The thought has crossed my mind to buy Chelsea a tire swing for her dressing room.

For some unknown reason, I seem to be one of Chelsea's favorite targets. Brad Wollack thinks she fucks with him more than anyone else, but he is sadly deceived. Brad Wollack is a whiner and an obsessive-compulsive, so not only does he talk about how Chelsea fucks with him more, he thinks about it over and over and over again while he counts the ceiling tiles and cleans his computer mouse with a Clorox wipe.

Brad Wollack

I also feel that Brad should be used to any abuse by now. I mean, just look at him. He's ridiculous.

I apologize to his parents, whom I have met multiple times, and who are lovely and very attractive people. Honestly, I wouldn't mind taking his mom for a spin around the dance floor, but I'm sorry, Brad looks like a newborn piglet with a red Jew fro. If you didn't know better, you'd think Little Orphan Annie had had a sex change operation with less than optimal results. Add some big glasses and a twitch and you've got a guy who got his ass kicked religiously in high school. I'm sure people have been fucking with him for most of his life.

Getting back to Chelsea...Just so you know what I'm dealing with, let me explain. Chelsea introduces me as a "little girl" to everyone, whether it's her family, new people at the show, people at dinner parties, or entertainment executives. I guess you could call that a lie because, for the record, I am not a little girl. I'm a grown man and a producer at *Chelsea Lately*. Even though little girls are cute and cuddly, they don't exactly command a lot of respect in the rough-and-tumble, dog-eat-dog, who-took-my-sandwich world of Hollywood.

I didn't really mind it at first, but then I realized that even though people probably didn't think I was actually a little girl, I could tell they were assessing my physique and thinking, "Well, he *does* kind of have an adolescent female body." "I don't know what it is about him, but for some reason I can't stop thinking about that robot girl from *Small Wonder.*" This doesn't give me the biggest boost of confidence about myself, everybody thinking that I have the body of a teen girl and that my name is Jill, not Johnny. That's also what Chelsea introduces me as, Jill.

If she doesn't introduce me as Jill, she introduces me as Baby Bird. I believe Baby Bird came from the size of my body and the fact that I'm not really a big eater. You wouldn't be either if you were looking over your shoulder during every meal, keeping your eye out for a lonely marauding basic cable host. I guess I don't put much effort into eating, and I will admit that when everyone at the table is finished I'm usually about three bites in. But what the fuck does that have to do with being a baby bird? It's not like I'm having someone chew up my food for me and then regurgitate it into my mouth. That happened only once, in Cabo, with a banana, but that was for a movie, one I remain extremely proud of to this day, titled *Drunken Jackasses: The Quest.* Netflix it.

The only conclusion that any normal person can come to is that Chelsea is infatuated with my body. She won't admit it, but come on, that's all she talks about. I'm sure right now she's probably somewhere thinking about my slim, petite body. Maybe she's attracted to little girl bodies and that's why she's always talking about mine. I believe she probably wishes she had my body.

Another thing you should know is that Chelsea gives me three to four wedgies a week. Not your cute, giggly, "oh, you silly goose" wedgies. We're talking tear-inducing, ball-crushing, bloodstain-producing underwear wedgies.

I'm sure by now I have the words *Fruit of the Loom* permanently embossed on my asshole.

This insane behavior is perfectly acceptable in the *Chelsea Lately* offices. How is this possible? Is that any way to run a television show? Do you think at *The View* the morning starts with Joy Behar emerging from what I'm sure is three to four hours of makeup, taking hold of an intern's boxers, and screaming, "It must be Christmas because I just gave you a Nut Cracker"?

But in this asinine workplace you have to learn to grin and bear it and laugh because, well, it's part of the job. "Ha, ha, ha, Chelsea just severed my left testicle. Hilarious." I know some of the writers can feel my pain and humiliation when she's doing it, but still they laugh along. I once saw it in Sarah Colonna's eyes, I saw the sadness and compassion for me through her giggles, but I don't blame her, she has a career to look out for. To this day I've never held it against Sarah.

Sarah Colonna

To mix it up, Chelsea doesn't always go for the wedgie. At least once a week she strips off other articles of my clothing: shoes, socks, belts. Ripping my shirt over my head is a standard. She will pretend to be having a simple, sweet conversation with someone, and then, out of the corner of my eye, I'll start to sense her slowly sidling up to me. I'll flinch. Then she'll start in. "What? Why are you flinching? I'm not doing anything. You're such a little girl." Of course I flinch, you liar. Why wouldn't I? You think Tina Turner didn't jump every time Ike reached for the salt?

Chelsea is a very strong woman, in almost a mannish way. She has the shoulders of an outside linebacker. Chelsea and I once actually met Brian Urlacher, linebacker for the Chicago Bears, when we were in the Bahamas, and I'm positive I caught him looking at her build with surprise and envy.

There are times when I'm in the middle of a skirmish with Chelsea, with my arms pinned above my head and my shirt pulled over my face, when I think she may have missed her calling and that she should have taken advantage of her surprising retard strength and gone into professional wrestling. "Now entering the ring, from the great state of New Jersey, Coslopus Face."

One of her favorite times to assault me is right before we tape the show. She'll be all dolled up, with hair, makeup, and six-inch heels ready for the camera. If I try to fight back at such a moment, she pulls out the "Don't mess up my hair. Watch out, Baby Bird, this journalist has a show to do." Standing alongside her, wearing bright red lipstick, will be her rather questionable lesbian stylist, Amy, yelling at me not to mess up Chelsea's clothes. Really? Maybe someone should tell Chelsea not to start a wrestling match in the hallway before she steps in front of an audience.

On occasion she has actually called to others for help in holding me down. Now throw in the largest lesbian on record, Fortune Feimster, who thunders out of her office to grab me. It's criminal. While she picks me up by the scruff of my neck with one massive hand, Chelsea rips my shirt off and displays it like some sort of washable all-cotton trophy.

I can only assume this is her pre-show prep to get fired up for the taping. A simple prayer circle would work for a more reasonable person, but where is the invigorating humiliation in that? Chelsea needs more, just like the ancient warriors who sacrificed a virginal goat before battle. That is, if they ripped the goat's shirt off first.

All this leaves me standing in the office without a shirt on. Wandering around at work topless just screams professionalism. That's one of the first things you learn in business school. It's hard to take a man seriously when you can see his nipples. I don't want to give you the impression that I'm not proud of my nipples. My right nipple, if I leave it to its own devices, will grow a single long silky brown hair. When I was in college I named him Harold.

Anyway, being topless on the job leaves me no other choice but to go to the wardrobe room to find something

This is me on some stupid yacht in the Bahamas. The crew offered to put Chelsea in a mermaid costume and film her swimming underwater. But because of my feminine physique, she insisted it be me. Thank you, Chelsea.

to wear. Unfortunately, for the fashion-forward hipster that I am, Wardrobe is filled only with crap for Chelsea. So now I'm stuck wearing one of Chelsea's tops the rest of the day. And her blouses are normally baggy on me. I don't know who this is more embarrassing for, me or Chelsea. The only saving grace is that we both have blue eyes, so a lot of her tops are somewhat flattering on me and have been known to make my eyes pop. This can turn your day around after being physically violated by a woman.

All of this may help you understand why I am rarely at my desk during the day. First, I'm obviously out and about shooting different segments for the show, but it's mostly because it's good to keep on the move when Chelsea is roaming around looking for a target. If I'm in my office, I'm a sitting duck. It's better never to be in the same place for long. But this brings up a whole other set of difficulties. If she can't fuck directly with my person, she will fuck with the next best thing: my desk.

If it's not a jar of salsa emptied onto my chair, it's steamed clams (without butter or oil; that's how she pretends to like them) in my top drawer. Numerous times I've come into my office to find my trash can and everyone else's trash cans upended onto my desk. I know it's not just my trash because I'd never subject myself to eating beef stroganoff before 5:00 PM. One day I picked up my phone and realized that Chelsea had cleverly taped a dead moth to the mouthpiece. I don't know which took longer, her delicately taping its little dead body to the portion of the phone closest to my mouth or tracking down the innocent moth and killing it.

Why would I expect her to respect my desk when she doesn't even respect me or, more important, my Cadillac? It's a fucking Cadillac. A vehicle that combines power, performance, and luxury should command respect. When I'm on the road, people pay heed because I am behind the wheel of an American driving machine. You might ask me, when I turn it on, does it return the favor? The answer is yes.

The first day I got it, I proudly took Chelsea for a ride

around the block so she could "experience Cadillac." First, she refused to sit in the front seat like a regular person and insisted on sitting in the back like *Driving Miss Daisy*, saying the only time she rides around in town cars is when she's being chauffeured. And you know what that big-titted, loud-mouthed New Jersey broad did? She hid two turkey meatballs in each of the backseat pockets in my brand-new Cadillac. Chelsea basically survives on turkey meatballs, arugula, and pints of hummus, not unlike an actual chimpanzee. Her brother Roy prepares these by the dozen each week, so Chelsea can try to avoid her natural instincts, which would be to gorge herself on raw meat and nacho cheese.

I drove around for a week with all four windows down at high speeds trying to drain out the stench I assumed had been left behind by Chelsea's own vileness. It wasn't until I had two actual backseat passengers in my car a week and a half later that I discovered the two dried-up Handler meatballs. I don't care if you hang a real fucking pine tree from your rearview mirror, that foul turkey meatball stench will be in your car forever. And even if by some miracle I could ever exorcise it from my beautiful Cadillac DTS, I still will never be able to exorcise the thought of her violation.

The favorite target of the abuse she heaps on me is my computer. To Chelsea, discovering an unattended, unlocked computer is like finding a giant bowl of dicks. She can't keep her hands off it. Until I started working with Chelsea, it had never occurred to me that I would need to lock my computer. Why would it ever cross my mind that if I left my computer unattended, some crazy person would use it as a device to demolish my life? I know why that sick bitch loves it. Because with my computer, it's not just a ripped shirt, stretched-out underwear, or baked beans piled high on my new *Sports Illustrated*. It's deep, it's personal, and it's devastating.

One of the things she does when she finds my computer unlocked is respond to my e-mails or randomly pick out a name in my contact list and e-mail them a message. This would be fine if she signed the messages, "Sincerely, Chelsea Handler," but what would be the fun in that for a deeply troubled thirty-five-year-old woman? No, it's much more entertaining to write a humiliating note to someone I haven't spoken to in five years and sign it, "Miss you tons, my cat died of AIDS, XOXO Love Johnny."

I think I should mention a couple of things here. First, Chelsea is an insanely fast typist. She's like one of those idiot savants you see on *60 Minutes* who can't tie their shoes but can play the shit out of Rachmaninoff on the piano. Chelsea can't sing, can't cook, and she looks like an asshole on the dance floor, but she can type like a coked-out court reporter with a plane to catch. I don't know why or when she learned to type like that, but my guess is that in high school someone said, "We're giving free abortions to the fastest typist in the room."

Second, Chelsea shows up to work every single morning

dressed from top to bottom in workout clothes. She pretends that after the morning meeting she's going to the gym, but I think she is just incredibly proud of her prominent cameltoe. She wears two sports bras when she "works out." Apparently she needs two bras so she doesn't beat herself to death when she jogs, but I know it's so her big fucking tits don't get in the way when she is frenetically typing and vandalizing my life.

These two things are what help to make her so incredibly dangerous that within seconds shit goes really bad.

Here's an office favorite:

Chelsea was on one of her "I'm bored" predatory strolls through the office one day when she found my computer unlocked. Since lunch that day had nothing in it that would have been interesting to smear on my keyboard, she decided to do me a favor and answer a few e-mails for me.

I didn't know what had happened until after the show, when I got back to my computer and found some e-mails from Kenneth Falcon, one of the senior vice presidents of E! Entertainment. I've never met Mr. Falcon, but his name always puts a smile on my face. That's because whenever I run across the original *Die Hard* on network TV, I have to sit through it to see my favorite moment: when the network censors have to figure out what the shit they're going to use to replace the profanity in Bruce Willis's character's famous catchphrase "Yippee ki-yay, motherfucker!" Wait for it, wait for it. Here it comes . . . "Yippee ki-yay, Mr. Falcon!" Exactly.

There's nothing unusual about receiving an e-mail from Mr. Falcon, because he sends out corporate-wide messages every day, about things that don't affect me and crap I completely ignore. But the e-mail I was looking at was different because I noticed it was addressed specifically and personally to me.

By that point, I'd been working with the busty habitual liar Chelsea for quite some time, so I was smart enough to realize that Liar, Liar, Pants on Fire had responded to one of Mr. Falcon's messages from my e-mail account. My mind reeled with the possibilities. What could I possibly have said to one of the senior VPs of the company I worked for?

I looked quickly to the beginning of the e-mail chain to see what my dear friend and boss had done to ruin my life. I knew she'd done something terrible, because if there's one thing I can say about Chelsea, it's that she never does anything half-assed.

I started with the original corporate-wide e-mail. Enjoy.

From: Kenneth Falcon
Sent: Friday, September 26, 2008, 8:42 AM
To: Office—Los Angeles Courtyard—All
Subject: Sunday, Sept 28: Wilshire Closed Between Fairfax and San Vicente
All—

    For your planning purposes this weekend, please note that the Israeli Consulate is hosting a major event on Sunday, September 28, 2008, in front of their building at 6380 Wilshire Boulevard.

Wilshire Boulevard will be closed between San Vicente Boulevard and Fairfax Avenue between 6 a.m. and 6 p.m. The planned ceremony will start at 1:00 p.m., and a large crowd is anticipated.

If you will be in the office or are scheduled to work on Sunday, please allow extra time to make it to the office.

From: Johnny Milord
Friday, September 26, 2008, 10:00 AM
Subject: RE: Sunday, Sept 28: Wilshire Closed Between Fairfax and San Vicente

Kenneth—I'm glad you sent this e-mail. Although I'm not Jewish, I have several friends who've volunteered in the Israeli Army and, through them, have become familiar with their tradition and some of their holidays, such as Rosh Kipper. I firmly believe it's our last line of defense in the Middle East. In fact, I'd be interested in getting your thoughts on which presidential candidate is better equipped to deal with this ongoing debacle. Hope to hear from you soon, Johnny

From: Kenneth Falcon
Friday, September .26, 2008, 10:55 AM
Subject: RE: Sunday, Sept 28: Wilshire Closed
Between Fairfax and San Vicente
    That is an interesting question. While I do
support Obama, I do understand that McCain has
more experience in foreign policy. I'm really
glad the debate is moving forward tonight and
look forward to what each candidate has to say
on the subject.

From: Johnny Milord
Friday, September 26, 2008, 11:17 AM
Subject: RE: Sunday, Sept 28: Wilshire Closed
Between Fairfax and San Vicente
    I feel exactly the same way. However, I do
feel like there's a lot more I could know, and
I'd love someone with more experience and the
same like—mindedness to kind of spitball with.
Do you have any free time over the weekend?

From: Kenneth Falcon
Friday, September 26, 2008, 11:47 AM
Subject: RE: Sunday, Sept 28: Wilshire Closed
Between Fairfax and San Vicente
    I'm actually in the desert this weekend.
Maybe we can hook up for lunch or coffee

next week. You're in the 12312 building
right?

From: Johnny Milord
Friday, September 26, 2008, 12:00 PM
Subject: RE: Sunday, Sept 28: Wilshire Closed
Between Fairfax and San Vicente
    I could come out to the desert.

From: Kenneth Falcon
Friday, September 26, 2008, 1:43 PM
Subject: RE: Sunday, Sept 28: Wilshire Closed
Between Fairfax and San Vicente
    It's actually a working weekend. My partner
and I are putting one of our places in Palm
Springs for sale this weekend and we need to
wrap up some things before we meet with our
agent Sunday.
    Let's shoot for lunch next week...Wed is
the best day for me as I can sit in on Tammy
and Lauren's weekly meeting.
    Let me know.

"I could come out to the desert." What the fuck did
he think when he read that? "I'd love someone with more
experience and the same like-mindedness to kind of spitball with." Why hadn't I just come out and asked him if
I could French-kiss his soft mouth during a steamy slow

dance at this year's Palm Springs White Party? Maybe in between the Appletinis and tea-bagging perhaps we could have discussed the complex situation in the West Bank.

This was not an ideal situation for many reasons. I didn't know anything about Israel or Jews in general, I didn't particularly care for the desert, and oh yeah, I happen to have an affinity for vagina.

At this point Chelsea showed up at my desk to see the results of her handiwork and to bask in her glory. This is the moment she lives for, and as soon as she saw the panic on my face she doubled over in uncontrollable laughter and peed in her stupid workout stretch pants. Whenever Chelsea laughs really hard, the veins in her neck protrude, her face turns red, and she wets her pants. Not a lot, but just enough to make it look like she sat on a large lemon wedge. I think she should get that checked.

So now she was rolling around in her own urine, crying, and gasping for air, and everyone was gathering in my office laughing just as hard as Chelsea. And to make matters worse, Chelsea's older, more mature lover, Ted, who just happens to be the president of E!, stopped by and wanted in on the sick fun. He came into the room like the dorky kid in the cafeteria who walks up to a group of cooler kids who are cracking up and stands there laughing along like he's one of the gang.

"What are we all laughing at? What's so funny, guys?"

Chelsea was laughing so hard she could hardly lay out the story between the tears, the drool, and the pee that I was sure by then had soaked her socks. When it became clear to Ted what exactly was going on, he immediately stopped smiling.

"No, Chelsea, you cannot do this."

"Oh shut up, Ted. This is hilarious."

Ted was adamant. "Chelsea, no! You've gone too far. This is unacceptable!" He was so animated that his middle-aged silver hair helmet almost moved. "Chelsea, you cannot do this to an executive at E!."

Apparently silly little e-mail jokes to the staff of *Chelsea Lately* were fine. Like when she sent a message from me to our newly hired production assistant, Ian, saying, "Welcome to the team, buddy. I love what you're wearing today. I think we're going to hit it off. What size shoe do you wear? XOXO Johnny." Ted didn't give a shit when "I" e-mailed the new production assistant, but when it came to corporate officers, it seemed Chelsea had gone way too far.

Ted and I were on the same page here, and I don't always agree with him. For example, I would never wear monogrammed shirts or get my jeans pressed. But he was right. This was unacceptable. Plus, I don't know if I need to point this out, but if he were forced to choose between Chelsea and me, I'm pretty sure Ted would fire the one who was not fucking him.

I told Ted that I would just write my now dear friend Kenneth and explain that Chelsea had a severe mental problem and had hijacked my computer. I knew it was not the kindest thing to do, because generally if I'm coming on to a man, I don't want to turn cold so quickly. That's never a good way to end a relationship with a man you've never met. I prefer to do it like a gentleman: in a steam room, wearing a towel. But if it has to be done, then it has to be done.

Ted said, "By no means can you ever let Kenneth know that this was a joke and that people over at *Chelsea Lately* are messing with him like that." In fact, he told me that I was going to have to go through with having lunch with Kenneth and treat him nicely.

What the hell? Now I had to go on a date? What would I wear? And who was going to tutor me on what the fuck is going on between the Israelis and the Palestinians?

I started to panic. "Ted, there is no way I'm going to lunch with this guy." Also, I didn't think Ted was taking into consideration that I'm pretty goddamn charming, so most likely Mr. Falcon was going to take a liking to me—and then what? More lunch meetings? What if that led to a dinner? Then, before you knew it, I'd be over at his meticulously decorated apartment when his partner was not there, and he'd put on some Teddy Pendergrass and open a bottle of French champagne. Actually this was starting to sound pretty nice, except for a few minor speed bumps commonly referred to as a penis and a set of balls.

Chelsea couldn't get enough of this. It was so much more mortifying for me than she had ever dared to dream. This was when her real evil genius kicked in and she said to me, "Jill, we can't let him know what you've done. Ted says you have to follow through with this. It's out of my hands." Thanks, Chelsea. Then she added, "So it's settled. You're having lunch with Kenneth Falcon."

I made an executive decision of my own and decided to pretend none of this had ever happened and hope for the best. I'm guessing Mr. Falcon made the same executive decision, because that was the last I would hear from my dearest Kenneth.

For the next few months I went back to the comfort of my daily routine full of wedgies and being called a little girl. I did wonder if Mr. Falcon and his partner had ever closed escrow on their Palm Springs hideaway or if I had negatively affected their relationship. Perhaps he started using me against his boyfriend when they'd fight, saying, "If you're not careful and don't start respecting me more, I have this sweet young man over at *Chelsea Lately* who is very interested in me and wants to know how I feel about worldly topics." But then I noticed that Chelsea had stuck my peanut butter and jelly sandwich to the ceiling and it was seconds from falling on my head. So that was that.

Then one day a mixer was thrown on our stage so people from the E! corporate offices could mingle with us *Chelsea Lately* folk. I wasn't planning on going to it, until some grinning son of a bitch walked up to my desk and said, "Hey, Johnny, that guy Ken is downstairs."

"Well, holy shit! Yippee ki-yay, Mr. Falcon!" Now let's see what you look like.

I needed to know. I had been this close to sharing an

intimate, lustful desert experience with this guy. I wanted to see if, had things worked out differently, he would have been up to my standards. I mean, if we had ever been seen out together, he'd better be pretty goddamn good-looking. I wouldn't want people to think I couldn't pull an attractive man. That would have been plain out embarrassing.

When I did finally catch a glimpse of him, while I was trying to look nonchalant, standing in the corner eating a piece of the delicious cookie cake, one thing stuck out immediately. He had a goatee, or as Chelsea likes to call it, a flavor saver. I don't really care for facial hair on a man, especially a goatee. But in a perfect world, I'm sure I would have been able to persuade him to shave it.

One final thought: Chelsea Handler is my friend.

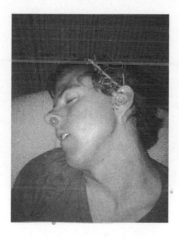

Johnny Kansas is like the sister I never had, even though I have two. There is truly no one on this planet I would rather spend time with sober, drunk, or asleep than Johnny Kansas. It's not my fault she feels abused and terrorized at work. That is the only way I know how to show affection. It isn't mature, it isn't right, but it's what I know, and it keeps everyone on their toes, or, in Johnny's case, her talons.

—Chelsea

Johnny, finally accepting his species and reading up on himself.

Chapter Two

Pap Smears and Punctuation Marks

STEPHANIE STEHLING

The first lie Chelsea told me was on the day we met. She was a new hire at the franchise wannabe Italian restaurant where I worked, and we immediately bonded over our ridiculously large families where every sperm was sacred and everyone shared a contempt for all things ignorant. Naturally it wasn't long before we got into personal matters.

"So, I'm about to be homeless," she casually mentioned while on a smoke break. "My fucking aunt and uncle are kicking me out."

"That's terrible!" I replied.

"Whatever. It's not like I want to live with all those kids and farm animals anyway." Chelsea's always had a remarkable ability to look onward and upward without concern.

"You live on a farm?" I asked.

"It's worse. At least a farm has the decency to have

stables. Those disasters keep the pigs in the house. There are so many children and so many animals, you don't know who is who."

"You can stay with me," I blurted out. I'd just met her, so I didn't think she'd accept, kind of like when you ask how someone's day went. You assume they'll say, "Fine," not tell you they've got a yeast infection.

"That would be great, thank you," she quickly responded.

Later that night, as Chelsea entered my apartment carrying two plastic bags filled with clothes, I wondered how I was going to tell my roommates there'd be another box of tampons in the bathroom.

"How long do you think you'll be staying?" I asked. "I mean, it's not fancy, but you're welcome as long as you want."

Chelsea and me. She was twenty-two in this picture, and my age is my business.

"Couple weeks, maximum," she replied, taking in the room's appointments, which were, as I'd said, not fancy.

We lived together for almost two years.

One night we headed out to a club, where Chelsea pretended to be Pamela Anderson to get out of waiting in one of those cattle call lines where the biggest boobs, celebrities, and attitudes were allowed instant access, and the rest of the suckers, like me, were left pining. Even though the doorman was adamant that she wasn't Pamela Anderson, Chelsea was even more adamant that she was, and so through the velvet ropes she went.

I expected to be left with the rejects when I couldn't pull off "Helen Hunt," per Chelsea's mandate. But always a loyal friend, "Pamela" demanded that I and my sensible blazer, scrunchie, and Payless shoes, which she had earlier condemned as "day wear," be allowed inside with her. This was the first time I'd seen her in action and I was immediately impressed. I watched as she knowingly smiled at her minion from our VIP table.

"Someday I'm going to be pretty successful," she informed me. "And I'm probably going to make a lot of money." Her nineteen-year-old confidence was infectious.

"Of course you're going to be rich and famous. You think you already are," I replied.

Much as I loved being entertained by Chelsea's harmless shenanigans, I was a rookie when it came to their execution. Once, she hooked up with some guy at our weekly Santa Monica stomping ground and ditched him shortly before the sun rose. Our practice was, if you met them in the bar, you left them in your dust, never to be seen or heard from again. Unless they frequented our place of employment, which this sad sack had the misfortune of doing.

"Fuck!" Chelsea grunted as she used her finger to stir some poor customer's iced tea one day at work.

"What?" I asked while stealing bites of some other poor customer's pasta. We were standing near the wait station.

"That's what's-his-name."

"Who?"

"That guy with the outdoor apartment," she said, finger-stirring another iced tea as we surreptitiously watched a not-too-unattractive guy take a seat in my section.

As she passed among the tables, head low, on a mission not to be noticed, the guy grabbed her arm.

"Hey!" he said, smiling. "I thought you were going to call me."

"What are you talking about?" she countered.

"Chelsea, it's me, Bobby, from last weekend?"

"Oh, I'm not Chelsea," she responded, her deadpan already perfect. "I'm her twin sister, Kelsey. Ugh, Chelsea is such a slut."

She walked off to deliver the iced tea the customers regarded as the best they'd ever tasted, then returned to me.

"If he asks, I'm Chelsea's twin, Kelsey."

The only problem in this situation was that I was not a very good liar. "What am I supposed to say?" I asked.

"Nothing, unless he asks, in which case you say I'm Kelsey."

"But your name isn't Kelsey," I pointed out.

"It is today. It's not that complicated, Stephanie."

The whole Chelsea/Kelsey thing was beyond stupid, but she was so committed to it, I started to believe she was Kelsey. I had seen her pull the same line on several other occasions when she ran into people she had no interest in connecting with again, be it an old neighbor at the grocery store, a customer from work, or someone she had accidentally fornicated with. One would have thought people would catch on to this, but, as Chelsea explains it so well, "No one would ever believe anyone was that psychotic."

"Just fucking do it," she ordered me in the restaurant that day.

"Okay," I quickly responded, wanting to get this right. Chelsea was the kind of friend who always had your back, so you wanted to be able to do the same. Knowing she was watching and expecting me not to fuck up something so simple, I casually strolled over to Bobby and offered him something to drink, perhaps a Pellegrino?

"That girl over there, what's her name?"

I looked around, past Chelsea and back to the guy. "Who?"

"Her. The one right there."

"I don't see anybody . . . So, that was a Pellegrino, right?"

"The one hiding behind the bread display."

27

"Oh!" I successfully feigned surprise, pleased with myself. "You mean Chels—Kelsey?! Goddamn it!"

I scurried away, passing Chelsea on my way to the Pellegrino.

"You are retarded."

Like I said, not a good liar. And when I'm on the receiving end of a lie, I'm a sitting duck. While I'm older than Chelsea, I've always looked up to her and have a tendency to believe whatever she says, even though experience should have taught me time and again not to.

Such as the time Chelsea called me with a very important request.

"You want me to do what?" I asked, incredulous.

"You gave me that stupid vibrator for my birthday and I think I hurt myself. I need you to reach into your coslopus and see if you have the same injury. I'm telling you, I'm really worried."

"Why don't you go to the gyno?" I asked.

"You got me into this mess with that thing," she not so calmly replied.

Chelsea had been very good to me, so I couldn't really say no to anything she asked. "Right now?" I asked.

"Yes, right now!"

"Okay. Just a sec. Let me put you on speaker."

And so I did. With Chelsea on the other end of the line, I pulled down my pants and started feeling around.

"What exactly am I looking for?"

"An injury. Some scraping, chafing, possible scabbing, and definitely something bulbous."

"Bulbous?" That sounded odd and certainly couldn't be good.

As I stood there, my foot on my desk, my hand inside myself with such intensity one would have thought I was spelunking, I sensed I had a responsibility to figure this one out. It was like a Nancy Drew mystery, but more awkward, and so gross.

"No, no scraping, chafing, or scabbing," I said, relieved.

For a moment I was overwhelmed with guilt. What if my prank birthday gift had permanently maimed my friend? The one who had done so much for me? I felt horrible. Until I felt something. Something bulbous.

"Oh, my God."

"What?" Chelsea asked.

"I feel something bulbous."

"You do?"

"Yes."

"Where?"

"Way up there."

"Then you need to go to the doctor and get to the bottom of things."

"I'm on it."

I hung up and immediately dialed my gynecologist. What the hell could be going on up there? Could excessive masturbating really do something like this? Cause a "bulbous" growth? Had I given Chelsea and myself self-diddle cancer?

Later, as I lay there in the stirrups, my super hot gynecologist investigating the situation, the last thing on my mind was asking him for the fifth time if he was still married. Instead, I just rambled.

"And I don't know what could have happened. I mean, it just appeared out of nowhere. I'm not even having sex . . . with anybody. Am I dying?!"

My super hot gynecologist emerged, doing his best to conceal a chuckle.

"That's your cervix."

"My what?"

"Your cervix. You're perfect."

Later that afternoon, when I met Chelsea to deliver the good news, she was laughing before I even sat down. That bitch had gotten me good. She knew what I'd find, that I would have no clue what it was, and that, in a panic, I'd race to my super hot gynecologist and make a fool out of myself.

"I'll bet you asked him again if he was still married."

I had asked him, but I wasn't going to give her any more ammunition.

It turns out Chelsea *had* gone to her gyno before calling me. And when she found herself in the same exact humiliating position of being told that what she was feeling was one of her internal accessories, she decided right there in those stirrups that it was the perfect opportunity to humiliate someone else. All she thought as the speculum was being removed was, "Who else can I make this happen to?" I wasn't mad at her; how could I be? How often does someone convince you to give yourself a pap smear while they're on speakerphone?!

A short while later we found out our friend Rose was getting married. We were happy for her. What we were not happy with was that along with her engagement came her conversion to a born-again Christian who never missed an opportunity to pray for our lost souls, make us attend pre-wedding prayer circles, and host four different showers. That her wedding was going to be a monster became obvious when she invited us to be bridesmaids by presenting us with handmade papier-mâché greeting cards that carefully explained in calligraphy what our responsibilities were and how grateful to Jesus she was for us.

"Who is this Jesus character?" Chelsea asked the group. I choked back a fry, shushing her. This Jesus stuff was serious to Rose, who was suddenly oblivious to the fact that Chelsea was and had always been Jewish.

Rose explained that she was concerned about how she was going to pay for her lavish wedding.

"Removing the word *lavish* might do the trick," Chelsea suggested. "You could do something simple and still have it be really nice."

Rose quickly dismissed that idea. "Chelsea, people are expecting big things from me."

When Chelsea and I left, she pointed out that Rose was expecting people to *think* big things *about* her. Rose liked to be the center of attention, and while we loved her, it could get really annoying. Nonetheless, we accepted the honor and did our duties with smiles painted on our faces. We also decided that in order to help her out, we'd pay for her wedding dress accessories, and we informed her of this via a lovely note on a generic, store-bought greeting card.

Chelsea said I had better penmanship, so I had to write it, but what we didn't realize at the time was that I wasn't good about reviewing my work for punctuation errors.

Later in the week, we watched Rose try on wedding gown after wedding gown until she found "the one." It was very pretty and very expensive, which was something we discovered when she turned to us as she was purchasing it.

"Okay, so you don't have to make the first payment for thirty days. Then you'll just make subsequent payments every thirty days for the next six months."

We could literally hear the seamstress's pins drop.

"O . . . kay . . ." I mumbled in complete shock and disbelief, not knowing how to respond to this turn of events. Chelsea yanked me into a dressing room as Rose reviewed veil options, which were also part of our new budget.

"What is she talking about?!"

"I have no idea!" I shouted back as I removed her vise-like grip from my forearm.

"It's obviously something you wrote, because I don't recall telling her I had an extra three grand lying around to pay for her dress! We're waitresses! What is she thinking?!"

"I don't—"

"You need to fix this. You need to say something."

"Me?! Why? You're the strong one! I'll just cave and end up paying for the honeymoon, too!"

"Well, I'm not going to do it, because I'll make her cry, so you're going to have to."

Contrary to what people might think, as much as Chelsea loves fucking with people, she has a big heart, one that prevents her from wanting ever to truly hurt someone's feelings. And this was one of those situations.

Later, after I spoke with her, Rose was hysterical as she reviewed the card for fifteen minutes. "See, right here." She pointed to the minuscule black mark between the words *dress* and *accessories*. "There's a comma after *dress*. I just don't know how I could have misunderstood that. I'm so ashamed," she wailed.

I couldn't take it. "Chelsea wrote the card!" I bellowed, at that point not wanting to be the bad guy.

Chelsea was not pleased with me for selling her down the river, not so much because I was inept, but because Rose made her attend extra prayer circles to pray for better lines of communication in their relationship. I should have known it would be but a matter of time before I had to do my penance.

A few days before the wedding, Rose announced that she had a surprise.

"You're pregnant!" Chelsea exclaimed.

"No, that's not something Jesus would approve of," Rose replied.

"I can assure you that if there is indeed a Jesus, he's not up in heaven strategizing about your wedding," Chelsea commented. I didn't have a fry this time, so I laughed into a pillow.

Rose put in a CD, then ceremoniously stood and announced to me, Chelsea, and the other two bridesmaids, Shannon and Theresa, that she was going to perform an acoustic version of Shania Twain's "From This Moment On" at her reception.

Three of the bridesmaids' responses were: "That's great," "Good for you," and "How romantic!" Chelsea's response was to walk straight out of the room. Rose couldn't sing. "Tone deaf" would have been a compliment. Nonetheless, we listened as she rehearsed, secretly wondering how she could be so oblivious to the fact that she was going to make a complete ass out of herself at her own wedding.

One night, after another of Rose's mandated dress rehearsals, I was in the restroom trying to figure out how to balance on my head the flower wreath she'd chosen for each of us when Chelsea popped in.

"We have a situation," she said, throwing her wreath into the sink.

"Did Rose find Jesus again?"

"No."

"Then what is it?" I asked.

"You know how she can't hit the high notes—or any other notes, for that matter? Well, she doesn't want to embarrass herself, so she wants someone to perform with her."

34

"Shut up!" I said, not buying it.

"It's true," Shannon added, her flower wreath dangling by a bobby pin. "She was in tears."

"We took a vote, and you have the best singing voice, so you have to step up," Chelsea explained.

"You think I can sing? I never really thought I could."

"Yes, you can, especially in the upper registers!"

"I don't know," I said as I thought about it. I wanted to help out Rose, but I was terrified of speaking in public, much less singing.

"Why didn't she ask me herself?" I asked, suspicious.

"Because it just came up and it's almost her wedding day. She has a lot on her plate! Are you going to help out your friend or not?" she snapped, irritated.

"Fine. I'll do it."

"Good decision. As soon as she starts the song, you're supposed to enter from the hallway," Chelsea instructed. "She wants you to really belt it out, especially the high notes. Don't worry, you're going to be great," she said as she slapped a CD into my hand. "Now, you'd better get rehearsing. You don't want to screw up her day."

When the blessed day arrived, the ceremony was long but lovely, and included several references to Chelsea's friend Jesus.

"Who's Jes—"

I elbowed Chelsea in the ribs, while trying not to laugh in front of two hundred spectators.

By the time the reception was in full swing and the

moment of the performance upon me, I felt prepared. I'd spent every spare moment learning the lyrics and making sure I'd gotten the melody right. Chelsea had even taken me to a karaoke bar to practice, so I felt confident I was going to be an asset to the team—until Rose began singing and I walked out onto the floor behind her, belting out the song. I couldn't tell which one of us sounded like a dying hyena, but I was starting to suspect it was me.

That's when I saw Chelsea, Shannon, and Theresa lose their shit. They separated from each other and split off into opposite corners of the room. I locked eyes on Chelsea, who was beet red and laughing so hard she was shaking the ficus she was attempting to use as cover. Was this a setup? Was I even supposed to be out there? I got my answer when Rose turned to me with a confused, deer-in-the-headlights look.

Leaving the floor at that moment would have embarrassed everyone, so I kept singing, trying as hard as I could to make it look like this was all part of the plan, and so did Rose, who wasn't about to let anyone think things had gone awry on her big day.

Later, after Rose saw her wedding video and realized what an awful singer she was, she thanked Chelsea for having me take one for the team. Chelsea told her she should probably thank Jesus instead, because she didn't intend to save Rose from anything. Her sole purpose was to get back at me for the whole dress/punctuation mark fiasco, which she did, because I couldn't hit the high notes either.

Chelsea, Shannon, and me at the ceremony,
moments before I sang onstage.

Several years later, Chelsea had successfully climbed to the top of her career. I was still doing the old climb and slide, did not have my shit together, and was kind of depressed. Chelsea suggested a night on the town to shake things up.

We were at a bar and she had just gone to the restroom when some ancillary friend of a friend, Chuck (a drug dealer), announced that he had Ecstasy. I had never done it, but when I saw how excited some other people got about this news, I knew I wanted to.

"What does it do? What does it feel like?" I asked.

"You lose your inhibitions and are just happy," Chuck suggested.

"I'm in!" I exclaimed. Chuck handed me a little blue pill, which I immediately popped in my mouth.

"You should probably take a couple more, since it's your first time," Chuck said, grinning lasciviously. So I did. Why wouldn't I trust a drug dealer?

Chelsea returned to the group just as the happy pills were starting to kick in. I began smiling and petting her like Lenny from *Of Mice and Men,* so she immediately knew something was amiss.

"You did what?!" she asked in a tone more protective than pissed, illustrated by the smack in the forehead she gave Chuck for giving me a tab of E. "Stephanie, you can't handle Ecstasy."

"I need this, Chelsea. I need to, you know, be happy for a minute. I'm not like you. I wasn't raised a Jew in a big city in New Jersey with things actually happening for her. I'm a guilty Catholic from a freak-ass small town in Wisconsin who *needs* something to happen for her. Please don't be mad."

"I'm not mad," she replied, then smacked me in the forehead when I told her I'd taken three. "Just stay with me," she commanded. "Do *not* leave my side, and do *not* kiss me on the mouth."

"You got it," I promised, then kissed her cheek, told her how much I loved her, and danced off into the middle of the crowd.

I was transported into a world where I didn't care about anything other than smiling, laughing, dancing, drinking orange juice, and telling my friends and random strangers how much I loved them. The happy pills were like fairy dust, their magical components capable of taking every dark thought I had and shooting them over rainbows. That was my perspective.

While I was busy being enamored of all things breathing, and imagining a world made of unicorns and gumdrops, Chelsea was being a solid Marine who wouldn't leave a man behind. Later, at nine the next morning, she broke into Chuck's apartment through the kitchen window and dragged me out. After we got to her place, she sat me down and played a video she had taken when we were all at Chuck's apartment. She had left me there for the night when it was clear I wasn't going anywhere that didn't involve penis, but made sure to be there bright and early the next morning.

"This is what you did last night. Are you proud of yourself?" she queried, then continued when I found I couldn't speak. "Under no circumstances is it okay to do naked cartwheels in front of anyone," she firmly stated. "I don't care how much Ecstasy you took. And Chuck? Really? He has the complexion of a rhinoceros's ass."

"But I had fun, right?" I asked.

"That's not the point."

"It sort of is—"

"Look at yourself. You look like you belong in a women's shelter."

She directed me to the full mirror in her bedroom,

which was covered with Post-its filled with obscure words she'd copied from the dictionary in an attempt to expand her vocabulary. Damn, that girl was always trying to better herself. Between *gelid* and *myocardial infarction*, I saw myself.

"Oh, my God!" I shouted. Apparently sometime before or after participating in my own rendition of Cirque du Offensive, I had slept with Chuck, who did have the skin of a rhino's ass, which had apparently been rubbed all over my body. All night.

She shook her head, disgusted as she applied antibiotic ointment to the myriad wounds covering me.

"I'm sorry."

"Be sorry for yourself. If you were still in your twenties, *maybe* this would be acceptable."

I considered this as she put a Dora the Explorer Band-Aid on my chin, the only kind of Band-Aid Chelsea uses. "You're right, CJ. Thanks."

"No problem, honey bunny. Now put on a bra. We're going running."

"I was thinking maybe I'd journal or something."

"I don't think it's a good idea to leave you alone with your thoughts right now." She sized me up then grabbed two bras from a drawer and threw them at me. "Jesus, when did your boobs get so big?"

As we ran that morning she grilled me about my career and love life, which were at that point both turning up big fat goose eggs. Even though she was doing what she always did, trying to cheer me up and help me pull my head out of my ass, it didn't work. The downward spiral continued, with a lot of partying, which led to a general lack of productivity. Chelsea was unimpressed with my lack of progress reports and suggested one of her vacations, which anyone with a pulse would enjoy, to help get me out of my funk.

"That sounds amazing!" I exclaimed, then proceeded to ask her who was bringing the drugs, specifically the Ecstasy.

"Really, Stephanie? After everything we talked about?"

"It's vacation! Come on, people are going to love it!"

Chelsea stared at me for a moment then let out one of those guttural sighs signifying supreme annoyance. She said, "I'll take care of it," and walked away.

On the day we were leaving, as I was about to enter the Santa Monica hangar where Chelsea had chartered the flight, she approached me with a very delicate matter.

"What are you saying? You want me to be your drug mule or something?"

"That's exactly what I'm saying," she calmly replied.

"But I thought you said you—"

"If you want them, bring them."

"I'm willing to do that," I quickly responded.

"Here's a bunch. Now stick 'em up in there," she said, handing me a Ziploc bag filled with little blue pills and directing me toward the women's room.

"Wait, what if I get caught?"

"I'll bail you out and hire you a good lawyer. Simone. Simone's an excellent attorney."

I knew her sister was a lawyer and assumed she was a good one, as I'd met her and she had seemed smart. "Doesn't she do patents or something?" I countered.

"Yes, but that's just a hobby. Her main line of work is international crime," Chelsea responded with a tinge of annoyance in her voice. It was exactly the amount of annoyance that I always knew meant not to ask any more questions.

"Okay, but do I really have to have them up there for the entire flight?"

"Yes. At some point everyone has to take one for the team. This is your time. Just fucking go."

I headed for the women's room feeling a bit nervous, but also like a proud renegade who was doing everyone a favor.

Once we arrived in Mexico and deplaned, I was feeling confident if not uncomfortable. A three-hour turbulent flight is made slightly less fun when there's a plastic bag up your coslopus. I was wearing a sundress and taking small steps, which I hoped might pass for normal. From beyond the security line I was approaching, Chelsea motioned for me to hurry up. I picked up the pace, all the while telling myself to act cool and be normal and just make it that last fifty feet. I made it only five.

In order to "hurry the fuck up," which was what Chelsea was now saying, along with waving, I expanded my

stride, which expanded the area housing the vacation con-
traband. In the split second I felt the Ziploc dislodge, I
tried everything I could think of to keep it up there, while
maintaining composure and speed. I even attempted Kegel
exercises, but only ended up peeing on myself and the baggie, which flopped to the floor right in front of someone I
was certain was a *federale*. He picked up the baggie, careful
to avoid what was either my perspiration or my urine, and
examined its contents.

It's amazing the thoughts that run through your head
when you're in a foreign country, with bright lights flicker-
ing above you and a uniformed officer with a badge you
can't read staring at you and holding the Ziploc bag filled
with little blue bippies that just fell out of your vagina.

I started thinking about my dog and how much I was
going to miss her. She was six, so I wondered if I could cut
a deal and be out before she got too old. Then I remembered how *Marley and Me* had destroyed me emotionally
and thought that maybe being away when she met her
demise would be a good thing. I thought of Vince Vaughn
and Joaquin Phoenix and Anne Heche and that movie
where Vince Vaughn sacrificed himself for his best friend
and the brother of the woman who was his love interest
and ended up in jail watching his best friend die despite
his sacrifice, and I wondered if I was going to be Vince
Vaughn or Joaquin Phoenix. And then I wondered how
long it was going to take Chelsea to get her international
legal expert sister across the border.

Suddenly the *federale* put the bag into my hand and smirked as he told me I was free to go.

"I am? I mean, of course I am. I didn't do anything wrong!" I shouted as I tried to stomp away. I felt like Wonder Woman but knew I looked like Bambi, my shaky legs contradicting my false bravado.

As I glanced over my shoulder I saw the *federale* whisper to a compatriot, and I could have sworn they were laughing. Once I returned my gaze forward, I saw Chelsea, who looked pissed.

"Get your shit and meet me at the car," she bellowed as she exited the building.

More terrified of Chelsea than a Mexican drug bust, I meekly climbed into the Navigator, hoping to sit as far away from her as possible. No such luck. She patted the only available seat right beside her. As I took it, I tried to look at the others to gauge the situation, but no one was making eye contact with me. This was going to be a long vacation.

"So, how'd that work out for you? Feel good about yourself?" she asked.

"No! It was awful! My life flashed before my eyes... and I could have gotten you in so much trouble! Your career, your reputation! I'm so sorry."

"Yeah, well, you should be."

"I am. But you have to admit, those *federales* are pretty stupid," I offered, attempting to crack her iciness.

"No, you're stupid," she countered, then turned to look out the window. I thought she couldn't look at me because she was so angry. That is, until I realized she was trying not to let me see her laugh. I looked around, confused.

"They weren't Ecstasy," she deadpanned, as everyone burst out laughing.

"But there was a little *E* on them."

"Yes, for Excedrin!"

"I thought . . ."

"You thought wrong. Do you think I would allow you on a private plane with Ecstasy shoved up your cervix? If you recall correctly, your cervix has already been through enough."

Chelsea and me when we arrived at the resort.

"So, I'm an asshole," I stated more than asked.

"Well, yes, Stephanie. You're thirty-four and trying to smuggle drugs in your coslopus. That is so 2008. Get your shit together."

Chelsea knew I was heading down a slippery slope that was taking me nowhere. Anyone else teaching someone a lesson might have included a stern sit-down or a time-out, but for Chelsea, it had to involve turning me into *Maria Full of Grace*. It was sort of a compliment.

I love that bitch, but to this day I sleep with one eye open whenever she's around. The best irony of all is that people sleep at Chelsea's all the time, and everyone knows never to sleep with their door unlocked. So, in a house with six bedrooms, a house that she paid for, Chelsea really has access only to her own room.

After reading this chapter, I've never felt more responsible in my life. It really makes me sound like I have my shit together, and it's only because the people I surround myself with have their shit less together. So, thank you. Steph's performance at the wedding was something I will smile about for the rest of my life.

I would also like to add my own photo to this chapter as a warning of what someone looks like when they dance on Ecstasy.

—Chelsea

Steph in Cabo, 2007. This is what dancing on Ecstasy looks like.

Chapter Three

How to Make a Marriage Work

HEATHER McDONALD

Ironically, Chelsea's middle name is Joy. This makes sense, as she experiences a lot of joy in her life, most often at the expense of other people. One particular instance that comes to mind is the only time in my life I ate a pot brownie. I am not a pot smoker at all and have never consumed pot, but I rarely have the ability to deny myself a tasty treat, and if there is one thing I love, it's extra gooey double chocolate brownies.

One weekend I was performing stand-up with Chelsea, and we joined some friends of hers in Provincetown for an afternoon boat ride. After a full meal and three cocktails in the afternoon sun on the water, nothing sounded better to me than a yummy brownie. I knew they had baked some pot in them, but I was thinking only about the effect a moist chocolate delight normally has on me, which is what I was craving after a salty Mexican lunch. So I did what I

48

always do when a brownie pan is in my direct vicinity: like a lady, I took a knife and cut off a sliver of brownie, and then another and then another. Everyone but Chelsea and the captain were eating the brownies. Chelsea is not a dessert person and is certainly not going to waste calories on even the best high, but what I realized later is that to her, the best high is being sober when everyone else is high and laughing at their stupidity. I'm a drinker, so I had never experienced the kind of high that lasts fourteen hours, like this one did. All I could do was laugh.

Hours after the boat ride ended, we were back at her friends' house. Chelsea walked into the room where I was lying on a couch, and looked at herself in the mirror. She was horrified by her outfit, which consisted of a tunic and wide-legged slacks, and asked me, "Why didn't you tell me I was dressed like a lesbian? I look like Paula Poundstone."

She *did* look like Paula Poundstone. She had had Johnny Kansas grab her some clothes after the boat ride, because she was too lazy to get them herself, but had never bothered to look at herself in the mirror. Her comments sent me into a tailspin. I had never laughed so hard in my life, and Chelsea was on the floor crying at my reaction.

The only thing that could have brought Chelsea even more joy in this situation was if she had been able to get it on film or take an extremely unflattering photo of me, high, with my legs spread on a couch, and send it to three million of her Twitter followers, with a comment that read, "Mother of two Caucasians and one half-Asian." Fortunately for me, she couldn't find her BlackBerry at that moment, which happens about three times a day.

As for the actual lies Chelsea has told me, some people reading this may think I am incredibly stupid, as I am often called by Chelsea Joy herself, but the lies she told me were all lies I was elated to hear. It never entered my mind that what she was telling me, as her steel blue eyes stared straight into my chocolate almond-shaped ones, wasn't 100 percent fact. Chelsea was not only my very generous and fun boss, she was my girlfriend, and we confided in each other all the time, so when she told me one Thursday morning that she was pregnant, I believed her.

I felt even more special when she swore me to secrecy. Of course, she was going to confide in me. I not only had given birth vaginally to two healthy boys, but was also a tender stepmother to my stepdaughter, Mackenzie. At the time, Chelsea was living with her boyfriend, Ted, who was divorced with two teenagers and pushing fifty-three.

THE GIRL WHO CRIED FIRST TRIMESTER

This is how it began. Every Thursday, *Chelsea Lately* provides us with an incredible spread, so we creatively call that day Bagel Thursday. One Thursday, as both Chelsea and I were scooping out the centers of our bagels—girls and gays, if you haven't done this yet, do it! You slice the bagel, scoop out all the carb-infested middle, then toast what's left, and pile on light cream cheese, tomatoes, and cucumbers, and a hint of fresh lemon juice. You get all the crunch and flavor with half the calories!—Chelsea casually turned to me with a plastic knife covered in cream cheese and said, "I took a pregnancy test today and it was positive. Can you pass me the lox? Why is it so orange? Never mind."

"Wait, what? Are you serious?" I whispered.

"Yes, but don't say anything to Ted," she warned me.

"It's not his?" I screeched as my pupils dilated two millimeters.

"No. Of course it's his. I just don't know if I want to keep it. Can you imagine if I had Ted's baby? He won't let me out of his sight now. Imagine if there were one of me in a baby form. Besides, I can't do stand-up comedy while pregnant. That would be disgusting. Really? I'm going to stand up in front of thousands of people eight months

pregnant jumping up and down doing my masturbation bit? I don't think so."

At this point I was still open to having another baby, and if I were to have gotten pregnant, I absolutely would still have done stand-up while pregnant. Why the hell not?

"Chelsea, just think of all the new material you could do on ultrasounds and having to pee all the time and the excessive weight gain. It practically writes itself." I imagined Chelsea with a Baby Bjorn strapped to her chest and a fat four-month-old with her same huge mouth looking out at me.

"Heather, calm down. Take it down a notch. I am not joking when I say I will not give up alcohol for nine months. If I'm pregnant—"

I cut her off. "Chelsea, there is no such thing as a false positive on even the cheapest of pregnancy tests. There are lots of false negatives but never a false positive. I once used one from the Ninety-nine Cent store that told me I was not pregnant when in fact I was already ten weeks along with Drake, but it doesn't work the other way around. You have to tell Ted. He will be thrilled!" I said gleefully, imagining gray-haired dancing babies throughout the office. (Ted has very sexy salt-and-pepper hair.)

"Oh, my God, can you imagine Ted getting all involved in designing the baby's room, bringing swatches of cribs and shit to the office for me to look at? Could anything be more annoying?" Chelsea said as she rolled her eyes.

"You don't get swatches of cribs, Chelsea. It's swatches

of bedding and wallpaper, but they have these round cribs so any which way the baby rolls he or she can look out at your view of the marina. Oh, you have to do a whole nautical theme for the baby's room with old-fashioned sailboats."

"Heather, if you tell anyone I swear I will—"

"Of course I would never say anything, Chelsea. I won't tell a soul, but I think it's really great. I mean just think about all the..." As I continued to speak, Chelsea just turned her back to me and walked out of the kitchen in the middle of my sentence, which is something she does to me a lot, so I don't take it personally, but what I was going to say was "just think of all the free high-end maternity clothes you are going to get!"

More important, Chelsea and I are roughly the same size. Well, her hips are smaller, but they wouldn't be after she had a baby. My mind started wandering with thoughts of convincing my husband, Peter, to have just one more baby, based on the fact that I could get all of Chelsea's hand-me-downs, both maternity and post-baby wardrobe. Once her hips expanded a little I'd be able to fit into all her designer dresses and not just her tops. Also, Chelsea's shoe size is eight and a half, and mine is nine, but many women's feet grow when they get pregnant and never go back to their original size, so I could benefit on that end, too! I left the kitchen shaking. I was actually more excited about the new office baby than I was about my delicious toasted cheese and jalapeño scooped-out bagel.

When I returned to my desk, I looked over at Fortune

Feimster, my lesbian/officemate. I was just dying to tell her my juicy secret. She loves babies almost as much as I do, but I refrained, and instead went to my keyboard and typed in "Pea in a Pod" in the search engine. I started browsing all the new maternity clothes, which were so much more flattering than when I was pregnant three years earlier and cuter than ever. If it took a few months for me to get pregnant, my baby would be six months behind Chelsea's, and if, God willing, they were the same sex, could you imagine the baby's duds I'd get from her? Chelsea is obsessed with morbidly obese babies; she'd be overfeeding hers like crazy, so the little fat ass would probably wear each onesie only once, maybe twice, before my normal-proportioned baby got it.

That night, before Peter had even poured my first glass of buttery chardonnay, I told him about Chelsea's pregnancy. He interrupted me with a "Will you just calm down? First of all, we're not going to have another baby just because Chelsea is having one, and she has said a million times she doesn't want kids, so she'll probably abort."

"Peter! Shhh!" I hissed as I looked around to see if either of our boys was within earshot. "Don't talk like that." Then I got back on track. "She just has to get used to the idea of how cute the maternity clothes can be. Maybe E! will build a daycare center in our building. Ted would do anything for Chelsea. That would be so convenient."

I imagined being able to use the carpool lane on the 405 Freeway every day from the Valley to the Westside legally. I currently keep a toddler dummy in my youngest's car seat, and if I'm really running late I'll actually take one of the children with me and have Peter pick him up later. With a real infant, I wouldn't have to constantly be looking in my rearview window for a cop while planning my excuse. I know if I got pulled over, I would ask the cop if his girlfriend, wife, or boyfriend was a *Chelsea Lately* fan, and God willing, they would be, in which case I would offer up Chuy popping out of a cake for their next birthday party in exchange for being let off.

The following few days I was so distracted thinking about Chelsea's and my pregnancies. This could be the glue that would hold us together for life. There was no way she would have more than one kid. She wouldn't let a mistake like this happen to her again, so her child would need a friend who understood the trials and tribulations of having a parent in show business. My older son already has two best friends who are both only children. Their parents invite us to USC games and to stay at their ski house and lake cabin, all to appease their lonely only child. When Chelsea's kid got to be about three or four, it would need a friend to go to the Bahamas with, and there was no way Chelsea was going to deny her child his or her best friend. Chelsea would spoil this kid rotten (see Chunk). So guess who would get to go on private jets to Atlantis, Cabo, and Aspen? That's right, me and my cute family of then six. Sorry, single Sarah Colonna. Enjoy your time now, because it is not going to last forever, and neither will your eggs—or, rather, your one egg by the time you read this.

On Wednesday, after we finished taping, Chelsea was walking down the hall outside the writers' offices yelling, "Who wants to go to Katsuya tonight?"

Chris Franjola rolled his chair out from his cube and shouted, "I'm free, Chelsea."

"Yes, I want to go," yelled Sarah Colonna.

"I wouldn't mind a little tuna tartare," stated Steve Marmalstein.

I love Katsuya. It's a super chic sushi spot close to the office. *My kids can wait another hour to see me tonight,* I thought as I yelled down the hall after Chelsea, "I can go, too!" Then it hit me. Chelsea was pregnant, so she couldn't eat sushi. The mercury in the fish is said to cause autism. You would think Chelsea would have known this, since she was good friends with Jenny McCarthy. Good thing I was going, so I could remind her to order some chicken teriyaki.

At the restaurant, before we'd even slid into our booth, Chelsea asked the waiter, "May I have a Belvedere on the rocks with just a splash of soda and a wedge of lemon please?"

"Chelsea, you can't drink. The baby's head will come out a quarter of the size it is supposed to," I whispered as we continued to scoot down the bench farther into the booth.

"I'm only going to sip it so the others don't get

suspicious," she said. "If I don't order a drink, they'll know something is up."

"So you're definitely keeping it?" I asked with relief.

"Keeping what?" asked Chris.

"My car. I'm going to keep it for another year," Chelsea said nonchalantly as she winked at me.

Oh, my God, my prayers had been answered. Chelsea really was going to have this baby. I was so happy. I love Katsuya and I love the Westside. Maybe by the time our babies entered kindergarten, we could move from the Valley to the Westside, since Chelsea's baby was going to want its best friend in the same classroom. Of course I would want to go to St. Martins, the Catholic school in Brentwood, but Chelsea wouldn't be down with that. Then again, Ted had been raised Catholic. Or we could send both kids to that amazing public elementary school I'd heard about on the morning news, where the parents sleep in tents the week before registration to make sure their kids get in. I would do that. Then my older boys could go to Loyola, an all-boys high school that is too far from our house now.

I was thinking how this was all going to be so great until halfway through the dinner, when Chelsea ordered another Belvedere and soda. So much for sipping her drink. It hadn't even been twenty minutes. Then she proceeded to eat an entire bowl of steamed clams, a plate of tuna sashimi, and a plate of yellowtail with jalapeños. I kept taking my chopsticks and eating as much of the heavy-mercury-filled uncooked fish as humanly possible, but as soon as a dish was done, Chelsea would order more for the table. At this point I felt full and pissed off. Everyone knows you don't consume alcohol or eat sushi when you're pregnant.

When Chelsea got out of the booth to go to the bathroom, I followed her, which annoyed everyone, because I was opposite her at the end of the table, so every single person had to exit the booth. When we got in the bathroom I looked around to make sure we were alone and then said, "Chelsea, seriously, you can't continue to drink unless it's after your fifth month of pregnancy, and only if it's chardonnay. I know because that's what I did, and both the boys seem to be fine. But you really can't eat all that seafood. It's been proven to cause autism, I think. What is your plan? Have you ever eaten gluten-free lasagna? It is not good. Come on, Chelsea, this isn't fair to Ted. It's his baby, too! You're already dealing with older sperm. How hard do you want to roll the dice with your offspring?" I was referring to a syndrome that started with a *D* and ended with *own*.

"Heather, I'm not pregnant," she said as she washed her hands.

"The blood test came back negative after you took a positive EPT test? EPT tests are the best. They're like seventeen dollars each." I was totally perplexed.

"Oh, my God, Heather. I didn't take any pregnancy test. I thought it would be funny to make you think I was pregnant, but now it's just getting annoying. Look at yourself."

"You really aren't pregnant? I'm so bummed."

"Well, I'm sorry. Come on, me pregnant would be the worst. If you think I can be a bitch now, imagine if I were fat and couldn't drink," she said as she pulled open the door and exited the bathroom.

And that was it for Chelsea. She never thought about that lie again or what a toll it took on my life for six days. As I washed my hands, I watched the soapy water slide down the drain along with my dreams of the in-office day-care, lightly used designer maternity and baby clothes, family vacations on yachts, and prestigious Westside pre-schools. I looked in the mirror feeling a little bloated from all the sushi and then suddenly remembered I hadn't taken

Michael Broussard (Chelsea's and my book agent), Eva (Chelsea's right-hand woman), and me in Cabo on a staff trip. These are the reasons we all put up with her shit.

my birth control pill that day. I immediately pulled it from the inside pocket of my purse, popped it into my mouth, and swallowed it dry.

DANCING WITH THE STARS

One of my lifelong career goals, besides securing a hair product endorsement deal, is one day to be a contestant on *Dancing with the Stars*. I work The Secret, and Fortune and I have a vision board in our office of things we want to accomplish. On the poster is a photo of Justin Bieber from *J-14*, a Pantene ad with that woman from *What Not to Wear*, and a photo of me dressed up in a *Dancing with the Stars* costume complete with sequins and a hot pink feather boa. Unlike other people in the office, I am honest about my desire to be on TV and believe that being on *Dancing with the Stars* would really help my career. I'm sorry, but I dance with my sons in my bedroom while watching the show, and the waltz does not look that difficult. Let's just say I'm not afraid to look to the side and walk backward. Besides, how cute would my kids look all dressed up and cheering me on in the audience?

So one day, in our usual morning meeting, Chelsea, who is very ADD but has never been diagnosed and therefore does not take Adderall, all of a sudden turned to Tom, our executive producer, and said, "And we need to get back to the casting director from *Dancing with the Stars* about who we think would be good on the show," and then shoved another forklift of arugula and hummus into her mouth.

"You don't want to do it?" I asked Chelsea.

"No, that show is a nightmare, besides the fact that I'm a horrible dancer."

Then Brad piped in: "Well, the obvious choice is Chuy."

"We already pitched him, but they can't take a little person because there are too many dances he couldn't really perform with a regular-size dancer," Tom said.

"There has got to be another little person professional ballroom dancer whom they could hire who could be his partner," Brad argued.

At that point I wanted to scream out, "Chuy complains about walking from the kitchen back to his office. He is not going to be able to properly dance the cha-cha for three minutes straight!" But I didn't. I also didn't say I wanted to do it, because anytime I pitch anything involving myself, the other writers say things like "And let's take a wild guess, you're going to play Sarah Palin."

Then Chelsea said, "No, they know that both Chuy and I are out, so they'll consider someone from the round table."

Oh, thank God. Of course it still didn't mean I'd get it, because chances were they were also talking to the *Daily Show* correspondents, but there was a chance.

Then Brad uttered the unthinkable: "Fortune should do it. That would be hilarious."

"Fortune, you really are a good dancer," Chelsea said.

"We all saw you at the Christmas party. You get a little too sweaty, but you have rhythm."

"Thank you. My mother put me in jazz dance classes when I was seven. I guess it really paid off," Fortune replied, grinning like a Cheshire cat.

"It would be fantastic," Brad said enthusiastically. "Think how much weight you'd lose, Fortune. It would be a total transformation."

"I bet they'd put you in *Life & Style* magazine and write about how you got your *Dancing with the Stars* body," Tom said.

At this point, jealousy was boiling over in me. I had started to shake a little when Chelsea said, "Okay, great. So, Tom, you'll talk to them?"

When Fortune and I returned to the office, she looked at me and said, "Heather, I know how much you want this."

"Fortune, don't be ridiculous. If they want you, you have to do it. Don't worry about it. But, honestly, I don't want to talk about it anymore."

"Totally understandable." Fortune put in her ear buds and began typing.

The rest of the day was very difficult. For a while things would be fine and then I'd remember *Dancing with the Stars* and get a major hollowed-out feeling in the pit of my stomach. When I got home that night and told Peter what had transpired, he said, "Look, Fortune is going to sprain her ankle or blow out her ACLU or something. This season alone they've lost like five contestants to injury. Fortune is bound to get hurt, and then they will replace her with you like they did when little Bow Wow got replaced with his dad, Big Wow Wow."

"I don't think his dad's name is Big Wow Wow. I think it's Master D or something. Anyway, maybe you're right. But then again, Fortune is pretty flexible, and being gay helps. Lance Bass went really far in the competition."

The next day in our meeting, the show came up again and when Chelsea said, "Tom, the people at *Dancing with the Stars* want to see tape on Fortune, so have Johnny film her dancing to something."

I started to tremble. *Speak, Heather!* I screamed inside my head. I wanted to say, *Well, can you put me on tape, too, so we can both be considered?* But I was afraid the other writers would jump on me and say I was awful for trying to take something away from Fortune, so I kept my lips sealed.

"Sure," Tom said. "We can shoot it after today's taping in Studio Two. Fortune, you ready to put your twinkle toes to work?" Tom winked at Fortune.

"Absolutely. Thank you," Fortune said and began to blush.

Thoughts tumbled through my head, everything from the fact that envy was a sin and it wasn't very Christian of me to wish Fortune bodily harm when she attempted the jive, to the principle in *The Secret* that there is no such thing as competition because there is enough room in the universe for everyone to be successful. I kept very quiet for the rest of the meeting.

Later that day Chelsea called me into her office and

said, "Heather, I know you're upset about Fortune getting chosen over you for *Dancing with the Stars,* but she is really excited about it right now. It's her time to shine. You know how I feel about everyone being equal around here, and you've gotten to do a lot."

"I know. I'm happy for her." What I wanted to say was, *Equal? Then if everything is equal* Chelsea Lately *is Communist North Korea and you're Kim Jong-il. Just give Fortune one of my dates where I open for you or a Cheescake Factory gift certificate. I'm willing to give all that up to be considered for* Dancing with the Stars. But instead I just left her office with a fake smile.

When I returned to our office to write our jokes for the daily topics, I could feel my lip tremble. *Please, Heather, do not start crying,* I told myself. I realized my period was two days away and there was no stopping the tears from streaming down my cheeks.

Fortune, who had begun talking about Monster Trucks, turned her head and noticed me crying. "Heather, oh, my God," she said as she jumped up and shut our office door.

"I'm sorry. I don't know what is wrong with me. I'm getting my period," I said as I wiped my eyes.

"No, Heather, it's a joke. *Dancing with the Stars* is not looking to cast one of us. Chelsea asked me to go along with it. Heather, you know there is only one star in this office," she said, referring to me.

I wiped my eyes dry and felt an overwhelming sense of relief. Fortune is the best lesbo/officemate I could ever ask for.

THE CHALLENGER SPACE SHUTTLE

The best and longest-running lie that Chelsea told me was that she was going to star opposite Meryl Streep in a movie about the *Challenger* space shuttle blowing up. It began with me in Chelsea's office before a show one day. I was doing my usual thing, which involved me smelling all of Chelsea's never-been-worn designer shoes. There is something about taking a Christian Louboutin up to the nose when that red sole is devoid of even the slightest scratch. Chelsea, who was used to this ritual of mine, was on her BlackBerry, barely paying attention to me, when she said to her makeup artist, "I guess I'm going to play Meryl Streep's daughter in this movie."

"What?! You are? That's amazing," I exclaimed enthusiastically. "You do kind of look like her, with your blonde hair and blue eyes. What is it about?"

"Meryl is the schoolteacher who went up in the space shuttle *Challenger* and—"

I cut her off. "The one that blew up with the whole world watching?"

"Yes, but it's a comedy. Meryl talks to me from heaven."

"A comedy? That is so weird. I mean, I vividly remember my teacher rolling the television set into our classroom so we could watch the launch, and then seeing it explode right before our eyes. We started saying the rosary and praying that somehow there'd been survivors. How can it be a comedy?"

"Well, that's why they want me. They also said I could add my own dialogue and scenes. I should have you guys help me write it. The studio will pay for outside writers," she said as she continued to surf the Web.

"Really? I just don't see how they could make that funny. A daughter losing her mother at such a young age while the whole world watched. I mean, I'm sure your character watched it blow up in her classroom as well."

"Well, let me know if you want to work on it," Chelsea said.

"Oh, yes, of course," I replied as I put the royal blue peep-toe pump back in its box.

As I left Chelsea's office I was very confused. I didn't ever want to miss out on an opportunity, especially one that involved writing on a major motion picture for Meryl Streep, but how could they make this funny? Then I thought about all the times I had auditioned for things and read breakdowns (a synopsis of the TV show, film, or role) and thought it would never make it, and then saw it go on to be a big hit. Maybe I shouldn't dismiss this space shuttle comedy so quickly. If Meryl Streep agreed to be in it, it had to be good.

That night I filled Peter in, and of course he thought I should go for it, because it meant making money, and not just any money. This was Writers Guild money and credit. When I tried to explain to him that I didn't think America would find making fun of the *Challenger* disaster entertaining, he snapped back with "Oh, the same way you blew off your audition to host *American Idol* because you thought it sounded like a corny show."

"They ended up picking two guys anyway, so I would never have had a chance." Brian Dunkleman, who was fired after the first season, was one, and Ryan Seacrest of course. But Peter's statement was true. When I heard that the show was about people from all over the country auditioning to be the next music star, I just couldn't see the appeal. I had clearly been wrong about that, so maybe I was wrong about this one, too.

A few days later I had a doctor's appointment and had to miss an afternoon meeting. When I returned to the office, I asked Fortune what I'd missed and she said, "Oh, we had to work on some more 'Who Would You Rathers' and, oh, they said we can submit ideas to be considered to write on the movie Chelsea is starring in."

"Do they have a title?" I asked.

"Yeah, *The Sky Is Crying*," she answered as she continued to IM a friend.

"Do you really think this could be funny?"

"I don't know, but they are going to choose one writer and it pays seventy-five thousand dollars."

"Seventy-five thousand dollars is a lot of money. Well, are you going to try to get it?" I asked him. "You probably know a lot more about the space program than I do, given that you're into *Star Wars* and everything."

"I don't know, but they want to see something in the next two weeks," she said.

As tempting as a movie was, and as much as I hated to give up any opportunity to make money, I thought I would let Fortune and Sarah Colonna take this one, even though I knew I'd get hell from Peter for not even trying. Then I thought that Chelsea's character could be a single career woman who could have sex only when heavily intoxicated, because otherwise the sight of a naked penis made her remember her mother's space shuttle. Meryl Streep would come down from heaven wearing the space shuttle outfit and give her daughter dating advice, eventually helping her overcome her fear of intimacy. Finally, in the end, Chelsea's character would come full circle and end up with an astronaut.

A few days later, in Chelsea's dressing room, while I was taking dresses off her rolling rack and holding them up to myself in the mirror, Chelsea said, "Meryl Streep backed out of the film, but they replaced her with Sigourney Weaver."

"Well, that's still great. She's amazing and actually she seems more like a teacher-slash-astronaut type, you know, since she was in all those *Alien* movies. I can definitely see her in the jumpsuit outfit."

"Did Guy tell you the studio is taking submissions?" she asked.

"Yes, I'm still thinking about it. What your character might be like growing up without a mother while constantly being reminded of her bravery in the sky."

"Now it looks like Justin Timberlake may be in it, too," Chelsea informed me as she applied lotion to her face.

"Justin Timberlake? Who is he going to play?" I asked.

"They don't know. They just know that they want him, but the good news is he's a huge outer space fan, so he'll probably do it."

"Like Tom Hanks. Tom Hanks was a huge space program fan. That's why he made that movie about Houston having a problem."

"I told the studio Justin should play my little brother, and they loved that idea," Chelsea said as she began to tweeze her eyebrows.

"Chelsea, I don't know if Justin is old enough to have been alive when the shuttle blew up. But maybe Meryl or now Sigourney Weaver could have had infertility problems after giving birth to you, so she had some embryos frozen, one being Justin Timberlake's character, and when the shuttle blew up, your dad and you were so heartbroken that he found another woman to carry the embryo and give you a little brother, and you see that surrogate mother as your mother, too. Then you would feel conflicted between talking to your real mother from the dead and the surrogate mother for Justin, even though your real mother is giving you dating advice."

"That's good, Heather," she said.

I was surprised. "Really, I was just rambling, trying to have this thing make sense."

"I like that she gives me dating advice, and maybe every time my character hears a sonic boom she—"

I cut her off. "She goes into one of many different

69

personalities. That's how we could make it a comedy. You developed multiple personality disorder after the tragedy, and things about the space program, along with different planets, trigger the different personalities to come out. As an actress, a comedic actress, this could be amazing for you to play," I told her excitedly.

"That is good. Start putting a beat sheet together and then let Tom and me see it."

"Okay," I said as I walked out of her office. As excited as Chelsea was about my ideas, I still thought the whole movie was weird, but at least I was coming up with something. Just as I returned to my desk, my phone rang. I saw *Chelsea Handler* appear on the phone's screen and my heart skipped a beat.

"Hi," I said as I picked it up.

"Hey, I really like your ideas about me having multiple personalities. How soon can you get them to me?"

"Can I have the weekend?" I asked meekly.

"Sure." And then I heard a click.

When I got home I told Peter how Chelsea loved my ideas for the movie and wanted something by Monday. My son had a game on Saturday, so I planned to write on Sunday. Peter would take the boys golfing so I could have the house to myself.

Sunday morning I got a call from my best friend, who is best friends with Kris Jenner. She told me that our whole family was invited to the Jenner/Kardashian house in Hidden Hills for swimming and a BBQ. You don't understand what a Kris Jenner party is like. It does not mean bring your own towel and have a hot dog. First of all, a Kris Jenner pool party is the only kind of pool party you want to bring your kids to, because she hires real lifeguards, so you don't have to worry about your kids drowning while you're busy impersonating a Real Beverly Hills Housewife with your back to the pool. She has waiters dressed in black, white, and pink, to match her patio furniture, and they walk around with an unlimited amount of Veuve Clicquot. This means you never have to get up off your four-inch heels in your mono-kini to refill your glass yourself. Needless to say, when I got this call I was beyond bummed, knowing I would not be able to attend. Instead, Peter and the kids would go without the matriarch of their family.

Around 4:00 PM I had made pretty good progress and actually had a loose outline for a scene where Justin Timberlake had reason to sing and moonwalk. The ingeniousness of it had me feeling I was up in the clouds, like an astronaut. I was about an hour away from polishing it up and printing it out to show Chelsea the next morning, when, being the procrastinator that I am, I decided to check my e-mail.

The fourth e-mail down was from Eva, Chelsea's assistant, and the subject matter read "Chelsea's Playboy Interview." I opened it and began reading. The interview was to be in question-and-answer format, to be featured toward the back of an upcoming *Playboy* issue. About halfway through, the interviewer said to Chelsea, "You do a lot of pranks in the office, I hear." To which Chelsea answered, "Yes. Some are still going on and the person who the prank is on is totally unaware of it. For example, we told one of our writers that I was playing opposite Meryl Streep in a comedy about the *Challenger* blowing up. Can you imagine? She believes that this movie is actually being made."

I could not believe it. I read the words several times. I looked up from the computer screen and yelled out to my empty house, "MOTHERFUCKER!"

About ten minutes later Peter opened the door with the kids. Just looking at his sunburned red face and still-wet hair infuriated me. I said, "The whole fucking *Sky Is Crying* is a lie. I wasted my one day off so I could work on this stupid thing while you got to frolic in a swimming pool."

"What are you talking about?"

I told him about the *Playboy* interview. "I told you I didn't think it was a good idea, but you are so fucking cheap you made me do it because you wanted me to make the money!"

"That's not true. You were all excited about it when you came home on Friday. So I let you work today and took care of the kids all day."

"Oh, like you're some amazing father, because you got to shoot the shit with Bruce Jenner about the 1976 Olympics while inhaling filet mignon and watching Kim Kardashian attempt to do a back flip," I yelled. "What an amazing sacrifice. You are so selfless. You should win Father of the Year!"

And then the thing that gets me angrier more than anything possible happened. Peter started to laugh.

For the rest of the night I attempted to ignore him, but he kept coming into the room I was in, so then I'd leave and go into another room, and then he'd come in there. Every time he entered the room, I'd yell, "Leave me alone!"

"Why is Mommy being so mean? Oh, are you sad you missed out on the gift bags?" he would say with a giggle.

"What? Who has gift bags for a pool party? Kris Jenner, that's who! You do know if we got divorced you'd never be invited again!"

"Yes, I do. That's why I really enjoyed today, because I never know when it's going to end," he answered, laughing.

The lost afternoon and the Trina Turk tankini and matching cover-up I would have worn to the pool party haunted me into the wee hours of the night. Peter did bring up several times that the person I should be mad at was Chelsea. But being mad at Chelsea didn't do anyone any good.

I feel more married to Chelsea than to Peter, like Gayle and Oprah before Gayle got divorced. In the last few years, Chelsea had given me better gifts than Peter, written me more heartfelt letters than Peter, taken me on more romantic and better vacations than Peter, and given me the most important gift of all—the gift of being on television. My relationship with Chelsea was much like a marriage, only better. Yes, like a marriage, it has its ups and downs. You have to take the good with the bad. What am I going to do? Quit *Chelsea Lately* and go back to selling residential

73

real estate because she lied to me about a ridiculous romantic comedy premise? Of course not. So, instead, I took my
anger for Chelsea out on Peter and am proud to say I have
not missed a Kardashian/Jenner event since.

The occasional lie or bagel and cream cheese thrown in
your face when you're not looking, solely for Chelsea Joy
Handler's enjoyment, is more than worth it. Plus, cream
cheese does come off pretty easily, except when it's in your
hair or in between your ass cheeks.

Heather is retarded. Period.

*Heather and Johnny in Cape Cod. Heather has her usual cougar glass of
chardonnay while Johnny looks on in disgust. It is 3:00 PM in this photo.*

Chapter Four

A Brother's Testimony

ROY HANDLER

C helsea first approached me about writing a chapter for her book one weekday morning on her way out the door to work. It was less of a request than a threat. Chelsea has a way of asking for things in what I refer to as "Al Capone style." The tone of her voice makes it sound like a question, but the look on her face tells you it's in your best interest to shut your mouth and agree to whatever she's requested, then promptly duck for cover.

Personally, I think I'm hilarious. I've been writing e-mails to Chelsea and my other siblings for years, but I could not bear the thought of sitting down for days, possibly weeks, and writing a chapter. My attention span has never been and never will be at full capacity. Then she told me what the book would be about: lies that Chelsea told me.

There has to be a minimum of five hundred lies that my sister has told *just* me. I grew up with her. All the chaos she is causing now was experienced by me and my brethren years ago.

There aren't a lot of things I do remember about my childhood because of my allegiance to marijuana. My fondest memories are of doing one-hitters in the garage, as it was the only safe place away from my father, who was also like Al Capone but worse. For hours he would sit in a chair half-asleep, then smell pot and follow the trail, which ultimately led to me. After that would come interrogation and screaming. I was always scared, but not scared enough to stop smoking the weed. One day, I was in the garage getting high next to a can of paint when I turned around and saw Chelsea sitting on a tire. I knew she wanted to get high, but in good conscience, I could never do it. Plus, she was only six.

I do remember critical times in the initial development of my retardation and Chelsea's ascent to the throne, such as one morning I came downstairs to get ready for middle school. My mom was on the couch with Chelsea and I sat down next to them. Chelsea and I spoke baby talk for a few minutes. She would always talk, but we could never make out what she was saying. Her vowels and consonants were not coming together and it sounded as though she were going through a Russian phase.

She looked at me and said, "Oyn oyn oyn."

I smiled. "Wow, she said my name—or at least she's trying to say my name." My mom smiled, too, and I was ecstatic. So as a good mommy and brother, we prodded Chelsea to continue saying my name until she got it right.

"Oyn oyn oyn," she continued.

"What the fuck, Mom? Can't she pronounce R? She's

not Asian; she should be able to do that." I felt comfortable cursing in front of my mom. Chelsea would later follow my lead in that department. My mom didn't mind if we cursed, as long as it was casual and we didn't use curse words as verbs or in anger. She told us life could be very disappointing at times, and if we were upset about the outcome of a soccer game or a D-plus on a math test, "Oh, fuck" was a perfectly acceptable way to express ourselves.

"Oyn oyn oyn," Chelsea continued while looking at me.

Simone, a soon-to-be litigator, sat down next to us and listened. Of course Simone, the smartest one of the bunch, figured it out. "Roy, listen to her. She's saying, 'You're a moron.' That's what she's saying."

"No, she wouldn't say that," my mom chimed in, shaking her head at Simone. My mom was trying to make me feel better about being insulted by a two-year-old. "I think she's just saying she's annoyed," she assured me.

Insulting us wasn't the only thing Chelsea learned to do before she could walk. Shortly after she started crawling, she would make her way to one of the bathrooms, untape her diaper, and throw it in the toilet. We just thought she enjoyed being naked, but once she got a better handle on the English language she explained her reasoning: "It's pretty unsanitary to sit in your own shit."

At dinner (food, good; conversation, not so much) Chelsea would bitch about kindergarten, then ask me in front of the whole family if I masturbated. I would bow my head in shame, lie, and say no, but everybody knew

*Martha's Vineyard, 1978. This is three-year-old
Chelsea in someone's above-ground pool. She had
no use for clothing—a sign of things to come.*

I did. We would pass all the food to my dad, and then
Chelsea would roll off a couple of jokes, which were funny.
Someone would inevitably fart silently, and we would try
to figure out who it was, then my father would tickle my
mother and blame her. "Oh, Rita, come on," he'd say with
a twinkle in his eye. That usually meant dinner was over.

Simone was the only one who could take Chelsea aside
and knock some sense into her. She would share words
of encouragement that seemed to have an impact. Glen
was good with numbers, so he helped Chelsea with business affairs and taxes. What business affairs a ten-year-old
had, I didn't know and didn't ask. At a certain point my
father had had it with Chelsea, but reform school was out,
because it was too expensive.

"Let her do what she wants and she will eventually come around." That sounded brilliant. Why the hell didn't he do that with me?

Fast-forward twenty years. I didn't have a care in the world, and things were going wonderfully. Actually, they were quite pathetic and everyone basically saw that except for me. I was forty-three, a chef, single with no children, and owned 33 percent of a house. The other 67 percent belonged to my sister Shana and her family. The obvious benefit of living together was that Shana's son Russell had a head that looked exactly like mine, and this caused a few awkward moments when we were introduced to new people.

One day while I was sitting in my third of the house, Chelsea called and asked me to move to LA. "What?" I said. "Are you crazy? The land of fruitcakes and nuts? Why would I leave my happy, pathetic life and move to LA? I love New Jersey and its culture. My whole family is here."

"I'm not," she reminded me, Al Capone style.

"No, Chelsea, I can't do that. My friends, my job, my life is here. I'm not ready for that kind of change."

"Are you sure, Roy? Your life isn't really going anywhere. You're almost forty-five, single, and living with Shana. Obviously, things aren't going great. If you come out here you could work for me, cook a couple of times a week, travel, and be on the show, which will probably lead to a lot of penetration."

"Okay. That sounds terrific. When should I come?"

I was scared, but I made the decision, and the rest of the family wished me luck, though I believe I caught Shana giving me the finger as I left. It may have been a wave, but it was very questionable nonetheless.

Fast-forward to California. Chelsea had just broken up with her boyfriend, Ted, rented a ridiculous house in Brentwood, and proceeded to move me, her Pilates instructor, and two Dallas lesbians into it.

"This is your new family," Chelsea informed me.

Johnny "Baby Bird" Kansas, Shelly (one half of the Dallas lesbians), and me on one of our golf outings.

I started catering for *Chelsea Lately* right away. I'd work there twice a week and pick up random catering gigs on the side. Chelsea immediately started putting me on the show and taking me with her on the road on weekends. I was getting more action in six months than I had in my entire life. Before I knew it, my bald head had become the characteristic that separated me from all the other guys on the show trying to get laid. People on the street were recognizing me, I was a burgeoning television star, and I was flying around the country in private jets. I felt like a Rolling Stone, only I couldn't sing and I was thirty-five thousand dollars in debt. Chelsea eventually paid that off, but not before she took away all my credit cards and told me I should be ashamed of myself.

Two of the people in Chelsea's life who never thought they'd see the inside of a private plane.

Chelsea's quest to find me a little bit of penetration hasn't stopped since I moved to LA. I appreciate it, but more important, I know better than to get in her way when she is on any kind of mission. I once got between her and a plate of chicken fingers and my finger still hasn't completely formed back to its original state.

In 2010, Chelsea was the host for the MTV Video Music Awards. Between doing *Chelsea Lately*, her book tour, and preparing for the VMAs, she had a pretty full plate. She decided that the weekend after the awards were over, she was going to blow off some steam in her favorite place to relax, Cabo San Lucas. I don't know why she calls it "relaxing," because as soon as her feet hit the sand she consumes more alcohol than David Hasselhoff at Oktoberfest. It's pretty impressive what goes down when she has a couple of days off.

Chelsea invited everyone who'd worked so hard for her on the VMAs: her annoying writers, her lesbian stylist, and her semi-bitchy makeup artist. She also took me and her fucked-up book agent, Michael Broussard, who hadn't done shit for the awards show but was fun to be around and a good backup in case Brad Wollack had too many shots of tequila and tried to put his toe in Chelsea's vagina, which, by the way, happened again on that trip.

Chelsea's makeup artist, Gina, and I had become some version of friends. She seemed a little distant when I first met her, which I mistook as her having complete disdain for me, but according to her she's "been in the business a long time, sweetheart," and tends to be "guarded." Whatever...She's got

This is Michael Broussard on our family vacation in Anguilla, but he was in this same bathing suit on that trip to Cabo. It's the one Chelsea wore on the cover of Shape *magazine. Several people have worn it since, none of them women.*

pretty hair and a plump pout, so I don't really take issue with her. She fancies herself a green thumb and also thinks she can cook, so I've spent a little time with her in both the yard and the kitchen. I've definitely seen worse things bent over.

One night while we were in Cabo, everyone got really drunk. Well, that happened every night while we were in Cabo, but during this particular night most of the group had trailed off. Gina had passed out, Brad had facial-ticked himself into a coma, Johnny "The Bird" Milord had finger-blasted some stranger on the couch, and Chris Franjola had disappeared at some club downtown where you could buy sex for less than two dollars. I had no idea where Michael Broussard was, but I do know that one of the resort bus-boys went missing for three full hours. The only people who were still up and drinking were me, Chelsea, Amy the lesbian stylist, and Sarah Colonna. Sarah may have been in a blackout, but at least she was still sitting upright.

We were staying in two villas: boys in one and girls in the other, although nobody ever slept in their appointed room. As you may have heard, Chelsea has some very ques-tionable sleeping tendencies. Maybe it's because we have a big family and she's used to having people around, but she likes to share her bed with random people. When she's actually involved in a sexual relationship with someone, she prefers that person to sleep in an entirely other state.

Heather McDonald had been studying Gina over the weekend and was working on an impression of the poor girl to add to her repertoire. In case you didn't know, Heather does borderline decent Drew Barrymore and Celine Dion impressions, and an impression of some poor girl who was popular in the '80s and had cerebral palsy. I have to say, though, that her impression of Gina was dead-on. Like I said, Gina has been in the business a long time. She likes to talk about movie sets she worked on in the seventies, and she acts as if she's met every big-time Hollywood per-son there is to know. I guess at some point in her life she

84

threw a fur coat out of the sunroof of a limo on Sunset Boulevard and told Heather about it.

That night in Cabo, Heather stumbled on to the patio where we were all sitting and was thrilled to share Gina's fur-coat-limo-sunroof story with us while doing her new-found impression of Gina. Chelsea laughed and then noticed that one of Heather's eyes was pointing off to the right. Heather is a pretty bad drunk, so Chelsea demanded that she go to bed before she started becoming really annoying. Heather stumbled away on her weird little legs, and the rest of us laughed at her.

"That impression is pretty good," I said. "She sounded just like Gina."

"Where *is* Gina?" Amy asked. "I think I'm sharing a room with her, aren't I?"

"She's passed out," Chelsea said. "You can sleep in my room."

"Wait, I'm sleeping in your room," Sarah reminded Chelsea. "Amy can go get in bed with Gina. I doubt she'll wake up."

"No, Sarah," Chelsea said. "Amy can't share the bed with Gina. Roy has to."

"What are you talking about?" I asked. "I'm sharing a room with Michael."

"Not tonight, you aren't," Chelsea informed me. "Tonight you're sharing a bed with Gina." She went on to tell me that she thought Gina liked me. "She's always talking about what a good cook you are."

"That doesn't mean she likes me, stupid. And, by the way, it's called a 'chef.'"

"Sorry, that's what I meant. I mean, you're a pretty good chef, but you aren't worth going on and on about the way Gina does. She likes you. She's alone in bed, and this is the perfect opportunity for you to go in there and bring your relationship to the next level."

I don't have a ton of self-confidence, due to the circumference of my head. When someone tells me that a pretty girl is interested in me, even if it's Chelsea, I want so badly to believe it that I just do.

Since Chelsea's friends have all been trained by Chelsea, they joined in with her. Amy started saying that she'd noticed Gina giving me the eye a couple of times while we were lounging at the pool, and Sarah said she thought she'd overheard Gina asking Michael Broussard if I had any interest in a long-term commitment. Pretty soon all three of those assholes had me considering changing my Facebook status to "It's complicated."

"Roy, go in there and get in bed with her," Chelsea demanded. "She'll like it. Every girl loves to be held, especially after a long day of drinking in the sun."

I don't drink as much as my sister or the losers she hangs out with, but I'd had a couple of sips of tequila that day, so I was finding what they were saying very interesting. Plus, I hadn't been with a makeup artist before. I had heard they're pretty crazy in the sack.

Even though I had already made up my mind to do so,

I let Chelsea tell me a few more times to go crawl in bed with Gina. "I expect a full report," she yelled as I got up and walked slowly toward my newfound lover's room.

About two and a half minutes later I walked back to the patio to rejoin Chelsea for a nightcap.

"What happened?" Amy asked.

I went to grab a chair.

"Don't sit down. You don't get to sit down until you tell us what happened," Chelsea warned.

"She didn't go for it," I mumbled as I ignored Chelsea's command and sat down.

"What do you mean she didn't go for it?" Chelsea asked. "We need details, Roy. Let's get serious."

I sighed. I was tired, ashamed, and defeated. "I went into the room, just like you told me. Gina was passed out. I quietly shut the door so that I wouldn't startle her. Then I took off my T-shirt and my boxers."

"Wait, what?" Sarah asked as she choked on a lemon. "You took off your boxers?" She, Amy, and Chelsea all started laughing hysterically.

"You told me to get in bed with her!" I semi-yelled. I don't really like to raise my voice.

"I didn't tell you to get in bed with her naked," Chelsea shot back. "What is wrong with you?" She then proceeded to laugh harder than I think I've ever seen her laugh. "What did she do?" she said, rolling on the patio.

"Well, she woke up and asked me what the hell I thought I was doing. I quickly realized that she didn't want me in bed with her—even though you told me that she did—so I panicked. I told her I was just trying to get some shut-eye."

"Some naked shut-eye," Amy said with a laugh.

"Shut up, Amy. What do you know about sex. You're a lesbian," I fired back.

"Roy, please continue," Chelsea said.

"Well, she told me that she'd heard my T-shirt and boxers hit the floor, which is ludicrous. Pants maybe, but who hears boxers hit the floor? She said that she knew I was naked. She told me to get the fuck out of the room and to stay away from her for the rest of the trip."

Chelsea was delighted. In her wildest dreams, she didn't imagine that I would have removed all of my clothing.

"It's not funny, Chelsea," I scolded her. "Now Gina thinks I'm a sex offender. We were kind of friends before, and now she probably hates me. I wonder if she's going to press charges."

"Oh, calm down," Chelsea said with a sigh. "I'll take care of it." She assured me that she would tell Gina the next day that she had made me get in bed with her. I don't know if she planned to tell her that the naked part was my idea, and I didn't ask.

"Thank you, Roy. That's the hardest I've laughed since I broke up with Ted."

I looked at my sister, feeling glad that I could give her that gift. So what if Gina started carrying a rape whistle around

Gina and me on the plane ride home from Cabo that weekend. You can see the distance between us. Chelsea took this photo and laughed the whole way home. Gina and I have recently been able to cook together again. It took some time.

me? At least my little sister was happy. As Chuy so wisely put it once, "When Chelsea's happy, everybody's happy."

"Just so I'm clear," I asked Chelsea, "do you still think she likes me?"

⁓

For the record: my brother is the horniest person I have ever met, and although I find that disturbing, it is one of my great pleasures in life to be a catalyst in his getting penetration.

—Chelsea

Chapter Five

My Name Is Brad Wollack and I Am Unattractive

BRAD WOLLACK

Me and Chelsea in a rare tender moment when she allowed herself to be vulnerable to my advances.

C helsea Handler is a hypocrite. The one thing she hates more than anything in life is a liar, and yet Chelsea lies more than anyone else. And not simple lies like "Brad, you were on TMZ last night—oh, wait, it was just a shot of Kathy Griffin's pubes." No, we're talking about emotionally crippling lies.

If she sees your weakness, she pounces. In fact, that's really the underlying premise of this book. The back cover doesn't say it, but it should read, "Here's the deal, Chelsea Handler mercilessly fucks with those around her. They all just have to take it, and here are some of their pathetic stories."

There are some of us she abuses more than others. Sadly, I'm one of them. It almost feels like I'm a recovering addict. "Hello. I'm Brad Wollack and I'm a constant Chelsea Handler victim." Chelsea knows all too well that I'm a psychological mess, yet this only fuels her desire to prey on my weaknesses.

Chelsea relishes the emotional strain she places on me when she fucks with me, and, truthfully, she probably doesn't care. For her, wreaking havoc on my nerves is a good thing. As long as she's letting off some steam, who cares if I'm contemplating suicide? And if you think suicide is out of the question for me, let me offer you some background . . .

Shit really started to go downhill for me at around age five. When I wasn't threatening to kill myself, which was most days, I would throw monumental tantrums for legitimate reasons, such as again being served chicken stroganoff made with low-fat yogurt, or my parents not letting me watch Ponch and Jon exact justice on LA's worst freeway criminals on my favorite TV show of all time, *CHiPs.*

I was sent to a psychiatrist at age six for regular sessions and I never again ate chicken stroganoff made with low-fat yogurt. After a couple years of weekly meetings with Dr. Hansen, most of which were spent with me pretending to be a pizza deliveryman and robbing the doctor, the best analysis the good doctor could come up with was that I was "too rational" for my age. What screams "rational" about a kid consistently wanting to rob innocent people? Even more confounding: Why was I pretending to be a pizza deliveryman when, like most Jews, I preferred Chinese?

That remains a mystery, but I do know that eight-year-old kids don't rationalize. For example, most of my peers didn't appreciate the fact that, while playing with model airplanes, I would insist that before flying, the planes taxi to a runway, get clearance from the control tower, and then proceed down a long runway before lifting off, front wheels first. Plus, my friends could never grasp the notion that there were always fog delays due to low-pressure zones at San Francisco International Airport—my hometown airport—and that flights would be delayed or cancelled. They clearly expected more from a playdate than just sitting there waiting for the fog to lift. Needless to say, I should have selected LAX, with its eternally sunny skies. I preferred solo playdates, where I could control the order and outcome, where everything was neat and organized. Plus, for the reasons just given, I wasn't anyone's first, second, or even third choice for a playdate.

Come college, it became clear that I had more than just a rationality issue. I was checking door locks religiously. At first it didn't seem like a problem; my school was in the gang-ridden South Central area of Los Angeles and it appeared as if I were just taking appropriate safety measures against the rampant home invasions in the neighborhood. But slowly, excessive lock-checking was complemented by constant hand-washing. I had become a full-blown obsessive-compulsive with skyrocketing hand soap costs.

One night I got in and out of bed twenty-eight times to make sure the front door was locked. I seriously thought someone was going to come in and violate me. Ironically, my new therapist told me that this was an entirely *irrational* fear. What the hell had happened to my rationality? I didn't think it was so irrational—who wouldn't want to rape me? I was adorable and extremely rape-able. In fact, I was the only guy in my school who carried mace *and* a rape whistle.

My obsessive nature stems from a family history of absolute anxiety and neurosis. I'm a classic neurotic Jew. In our defense, Jews have been fucked with so many times throughout history that I think it's okay to be a little on edge. I'm always apprehensive when getting on a train or

93

into a shower. In fact, I am anxious 24/7. As a result, I'm heavily medicated. I have been on a steady dose of antidepressants since I was twenty. In theory, the pills control my anxiety and depression. (Suicide runs in my family, and that just kills me.) Fortunately for me, my anxiety isn't just manifested by compulsions. I also exhibit a wide range of tics and twitches; so much so that I self-diagnosed myself with Tourette's because it's just easier to explain. You should know that it's not the kind of Tourette's that makes one swear uncontrollably. I just happen to like profanity and use it often.

My bodily twitches are always morphing. There is the constant teeth grinding and jaw clenching, and, currently, I'm gnawing on the inside of my left cheek, which is causing a widening wound that's the size of Kate Gosselin's vagina. I also blink my eyes rapidly, drying them out, and flex the veins in my neck, which makes me look like a Velociraptor. Or at least a Velociraptor that's had a stroke and whose mouth is pulled back at the side. It's really unattractive . . . especially when I'm making love.

In fifth grade I got in trouble once for raising my eyebrows—my twitch of choice at the time—at my teacher. She thought I was flirting with her. How she even thought that, I will never know. I was (and still am) a clean freak, and she was a hippie teacher who worked in the Peace Corps in Nepal and had hairy underarms. Fucking gross . . . and that's just concerning the Peace Corps.

My twitches aren't lost on Chelsea. She thinks they are

hilarious and is constantly noting new ones. But rather than being sympathetic, she attempts to mimic the twitch for comedic effect. She'll usually do this when I come into her office to talk about something personal or request a day off. In the middle of a serious conversation she will start squinting her eyes uncontrollably and exaggeratedly and then start gnawing on her lower lip.

Now that you understand my emotional fragility, you can better assess the psychological toll Chelsea and her lies take on me and my weak mental state. I'm incredibly insecure, and she has no trouble exploiting that.

In truth, her lies start innocently enough, kind of like one of those guys pretending to be a teenage girl in a chat room. At a party once, she said she was going to the bathroom and hadn't returned after twenty minutes. I thought she was taking a massive dump, but she had slipped out the back door. At another gathering, she insisted on driving me home because I was "too drunk," but she just wanted to get away from a creepy guy who was trying to aggressively pet her. Turns out, she ended up dating that "creepy guy" for four years.

Don't get me wrong. Her lies can be hilarious, but not when you're the poor pawn in her cruel game. Just this past year several of us were on a vacation in Napa Valley. My wife, Shannon, and I were staying with my parents at their home, while Chelsea, Johnny Kansas, and the Texas lesbians were staying at a high-end luxury resort. Their hotel had a strict "no dog" policy, which Chelsea found out when she called to reserve the room and inquired about bringing her dog, Chunk. She felt so bad about leaving Chunk at home most every weekend while on tour, so despite the resort's policy, she opted to bring him that weekend anyway.

Chunk was sneaked into her room and didn't cause a problem until the final night. After a debauched evening of drinking and smoking weed provided to us by one of the resort employees, we got hungry at around two in the morning and ordered some room service. Too high to recall the stringent no-pet policy—and too hungry to care—we carelessly opened the door without any concern when room service arrived. No one seemed to remember that a large, dopey German shepherd/chow mutt might alarm hotel staff. Chunk, clearly not aware of the anti-pet policy, trotted into the main room of the suite to greet the server and inquire about his own order.

"Is this your dog?" the hotel employee inquired.

The rest of us were dumbfounded, entirely ill equipped to answer the question. We'd been busted. No way out of this. I picked up my iPhone and started dialing the local cab company, knowing we were about to get kicked to the curb and that none of us would be able to drive back to my parents' house in our condition. But Chelsea didn't miss a beat.

"No, not at all," Chelsea said, sounding concerned. "We just found him wandering the parking lot, lost and scared, and we brought him in, poor thing." Then she turned toward Chunk, got on one knee, and said, "What's your name, little puppy? I think he must be lost." She turned back to the hotel employee and said, with a completely straight face, "I don't even know if this is a dog. It might be a cat."

I was stunned, and it took all my might to keep from laughing. There was no way this guy would believe that. First of all, Chunk is clearly a dog. He was also perfectly groomed, had dog tags, and looked totally at home in the room. Plus, how many guests at a five-star resort, upon finding a one-hundred-pound stray dog, instead of calling the front desk, bother to take it in and put it up for the evening?

The man stared at Chelsea. I was sure we were busted. But all he said was, "Oh, okay. That was nice of you. If you need any assistance with the dog . . . or the cat in the morning, let us know."

Either he was the biggest idiot ever, or Chelsea Handler is the best liar in the world. As I've found out on several occasions, it's definitely the latter. And the following lies have permanently scarred me.

JOHNNY MOVES IN

Chelsea is one of the most impatient people I know, but when it comes to playing pranks, she has nothing but time. She'll let things fester forever. A lot of times she starts a lie and then actually forgets about it, leading someone to believe a falsehood for months or even years. Even if she doesn't forget it, she rarely, if ever, has an expiration date or an end to a prank. She'll just let it linger...

If you watch *Chelsea Lately* regularly or follow Chelsea on Twitter, you are very well aware of Johnny "Kansas" Milord, aka The Bird. Chelsea dubbed him The Bird because of his frail frame and the way he eats: he kind of just pecks at his food. In truth, I've never even seen him finish a meal. He looks like a little girl.

Johnny is a lovable little guy, and Chelsea has always had a soft spot for him. Personally, I think they are in love, but Chelsea thinks I'm retarded. She actually thinks I'm retarded for a lot of reasons, not just because I'm convinced she wants to make babies with Johnny.

Johnny eating his lunch at the office. I mean, really.

Regardless, Johnny can be a mess. He always drinks too much and is a nervous wreck, but unlike me, who externalizes all of my thoughts and concerns, Johnny internalizes and frets over everything. That's why he's twenty-nine and has already had an ulcer. He can't make a decision to save his life.

So, a month into the start of *Chelsea Lately*, after Chelsea told me that Johnny's apartment had flooded and he was temporarily moving in with her and her boyfriend, Ted—the CEO of our network, E!—I didn't think twice. Of course Johnny's apartment had flooded; he lived in some shitbox on the east side of Los Angeles. After the flood, he had no game plan as to where to move to or what to do. He had to let Chelsea dictate all of that for him.

Even though Johnny's submissive, I was still surprised that he accepted Chelsea's offer to move in with her and, in effect, his big boss, Ted. It's a bit odd, but knowing Chelsea, I'm sure she insisted that he stay with them. She always has people staying with her. She'll have the most random people crash with her, most of the time even in her own bed. She's basically become the Michael Jackson of comedy.

A couple of nights into Johnny's stay and all seemed fine. I was really curious about the specific living arrangements and how everything in the house was playing out. After all, this wasn't a little weekend getaway for Johnny; he was full-on living with his bosses. That meant sleeping, meals, laundry, etc.

From the outset, I was so uncomfortable with this setup that I needed to know every detail. For example, what did Johnny sleep in? I, for one, sleep in boxers and nothing else (that's right, ladies, start visualizing). But I'm not sure I could wear just boxers while residing in someone else's home. What if there were a midnight fire alarm, an earthquake, or an early morning visit from the Breakfast Burrito truck and everyone had to get outside quickly? It would have been a little inappropriate if Johnny came running out in underwear and nothing else. How would they take him—and his girlish figure—seriously at the office the next day? That could negatively reflect on his capabilities as an employee. Besides, in someone else's pad, you must be ready for anything. In fact, in this situation, I'd sleep in jeans so I could be prepared for whatever went down. Perhaps a sweatshirt, too. My nipples harden quickly in the cold air.

At every chance I got, I expressed my discomfort with the arrangement, but Chelsea insisted that this was standard operating procedure and made me sound like I was the idiot.

"Brad, it's not that big a deal. He stays in the guest room, wears boxers and a T-shirt, and, yes, we have dinner together every night."

I was a little disappointed in Johnny's choice of sleepwear, but it wasn't my place to correct him. One morning Chelsea said, "Ted makes breakfast for everyone. Johnny loves Ted's oatmeal." That's stupid. Who has a special oatmeal recipe? (By the way, if someone were to have a special oatmeal recipe, it would be Ted Harbert.)

As days turned into two weeks, any comfort I had with this deal completely subsided. This was not healthy and it couldn't end well. Johnny was getting too intimate with his bosses.

I began assessing how I would have handled the situation if I had been Johnny. First, I would most likely have tried to get the landlord of my flooded building to pay for a hotel for me, or at least crashed at a buddy's place. In my obsessive mind, I can't get comfortable staying in someone's home unless they are a direct relative or an old friend. I always feel like it's an imposition and that the person hates me and resents my existence. I even feel like that at home with my wife at times, but that's another book. I think it's a reflection on how I would feel if someone I wasn't close to stayed with me: What the fuck are you doing here? Don't touch my shit, and did you pick up my dry cleaning? They'd have to earn their room and board.

I constantly asked Johnny how long he planned on staying with Chelsea and Ted, yet he couldn't give me a straight answer. "I don't know" was his standard response. I was livid; how could he not know? It's not like he'd been displaced by Hurricane Katrina and lost all his worldly goods and maybe even a few family members. There'd been a little flood in his shitbox of a studio apartment. This didn't require FEMA-type relief. For some reason, I needed a timeline for exactly how long Johnny planned on shacking up with his boss. This couldn't be an open-ended stay; that was just not appropriate. And while Johnny, in my mind, had already done the unthinkable and accepted Chelsea's invitation, I knew that he was a good kid with good manners and he'd never overstay his welcome.

I pressed him further. Was this stay going to last another week? Another two weeks? A month? When he refused to give me a hard-and-fast date, I became preoccupied with calculating the amount of time—based on Johnny's description of what had happened to his apartment—it would take for his landlord to fix the flood damage.

As a Jew who never does manual labor, I could have been slightly off in my calculations, but assuming they had stopped the gush of water in Johnny's crappy studio apartment, I figured the whole process couldn't take longer than two weeks. Again, I'm not a contractor, but I have certain expectations and know the timeline I would have accepted.

I impressed this upon Johnny, but he couldn't be bothered. How was he not concerned with how long he was going to be put out? He was effectively homeless. He had some clothes and that was about it. Didn't he want to go home to his things and his own space? Even if the remodel was going to take a year, he couldn't realistically think he was going to live with Chelsea and Ted the whole time, could he? What kind of a sick world were we living in?

It wasn't even so much his overstaying his welcome with Chelsea that concerned me. Because of her age, relative immaturity, and obsession with Johnny, she was much more of a peer than a boss to him. What I was fixated on was how Johnny could live with *Ted*. After all, Ted is somewhat of a legend in the TV landscape. He ran ABC and NBC studios and is considered a big-time television executive. I mean, he was the guy responsible for such hits as *Boy Meets World*. To an up-and-coming producer like Johnny, it was best not to overstep his boundaries with a guy like Ted, but Johnny seemed to have no concerns.

In truth, I was actually a little envious of Johnny getting so much face time with Harbert. I relished any one-on-one time with Ted so I could pepper him with questions about the industry. Now here was Johnny going to sleep in his boxers and T-shirt and waking up with the guy. In my mind, his future as a successful TV producer was a lock. I was now obsessed with assuming that Johnny was quickly becoming Ted's "guy."

If you think I was overreacting, then you're right, I probably was, but Johnny and Ted's relationship was rapidly blossoming. Stories of their camaraderie were making me sick.

First came Chelsea's announcement at a meeting that Ted had gone into Johnny's room that morning and said, "I'm doing a load of laundry. Do you have any colors, Johnny?" Really? Johnny was letting his host, the CEO of Comcast Entertainment, do his dirty laundry? I started to twitch.

Then came the dinner at Katsuya, Chelsea's favorite LA restaurant. It was a Thursday night, and my wife and I were there with Chelsea, Ted, and another couple. I was conveniently situated at one end of the table, next to Ted, and hoped to capture some wisdom or insight from him. Ted loved answering my questions, and I saw this as a chance to reassert myself as his number one. I always had this weird fantasy that I'd say something so profound that he'd respond with "You're right, Brad. That's genius!" and anoint me as his new programming guru and I'd become his most trusted adviser. In reality, I usually ended up getting drunk and passing out. Yet I always clung to that dream.

We'd been seated for fifteen minutes when Ted's cell phone rang. He looked at his screen. "Oh, it's Johnny. Hold on." With that, he answered the phone. "Hey, Johnny. What's up?"

Wow, I thought, *I can't believe Johnny has the fucking nerve to call during dinner.* What was so important that Johnny, knowing full well that Ted was out to dinner, would call him? It had to be a critical, time-sensitive matter . . . something like Ryan Seacrest wanting to refrost his hair and needing Ted's approval on the color scheme. Johnny hates imposing on anyone at any time, so he would never be so forward as to interrupt someone's dinner.

"You want to watch a DVD in the living room?" Ted asked. "Sure, I'll walk you through how to do that."

Unreal! That took major balls to call and ask something like that.

"Oh, that's cute," Chelsea said. "He wants to watch a DVD."

That's not "cute." That's obnoxious. Figure it out yourself, Johnny. Suddenly I envisioned Johnny lounging around Ted and Chelsea's condo like a sloth, probably in his underwear, helping himself to popcorn and whatever booze they had, wanting to watch a DVD. I couldn't believe he had the audacity to call with such a concern. If I were Johnny, I'd have sat in total fucking silence until they got home. But no, not Johnny Kansas. He wanted his DVD on demand and had no qualms about ringing up ol' CEO Teddy and asking him to put down his Tuna with Crispy Rice sushi to walk him through the process of starting a DVD on a sixty-inch HDTV. Johnny was getting too comfortable, and I was fuming.

"What DVD do you want to watch?...Oh, that's a good one," Ted assured Johnny. I was beside myself. Ted was not only unperturbed by the interruption, but he'd actually offered Johnny kudos on the DVD selection he'd just made! He suddenly admired Johnny's taste. All sorts of assumptions ran through my head about how Ted and Johnny would start their own guys' movie night and discuss the films afterward, Ted anxiously awaiting Johnny's honest feedback because he "always has the most refreshing perspective on things."

How could this be happening? How was Johnny getting away with being so brash? The only rationale I could conjure up was that Chelsea loved Johnny, and that Ted was so in love with Chelsea he would accommodate any of her demands, including allowing an employee to live with them. If Chelsea was cool with it, so was Ted. It was a demented love triangle...and someone was going to wind up hurt.

I was having immense trouble coming to terms with this situation. As long as I had known Johnny, he had never wanted to overstep his bounds or inflict his presence on anyone. If anything, there had always been a lot of me telling him, "Don't be a pussy. Just do it!" Add to all of this the fact that Chelsea was his boss so he now lived with both of their bosses, and I felt totally distressed on Johnny's behalf. This was *not* going to end well.

Two full months in and Johnny was still living with Chelsea and Ted. I questioned Johnny every now and again and he was rather dismissive. I had graduated from being a concerned friend to a guy who thought Johnny was just blatantly rude. I kept inquiring about the status of the renovations on his apartment, and he'd just say they were still working on it. He didn't seem to mind. Wasn't he paying rent? Didn't he want to go home? Didn't he feel uncomfortable in someone else's house?

Over the next couple of months, Johnny progressed from house guest to full-fledged family member who was factored into every major decision.

"Of course Johnny's coming with us to St. Barths over Christmas," Chelsea assured me one morning. "He lives with us, Brad."

I couldn't contain my surprise. "He's staying with you *temporarily*, Chelsea. You don't have to bring him on vacation. He's not your child."

"He is our child, Brad. And you need to start dealing with it."

It was at this moment that she felt compelled to offer me the grand perspective on her relationship with Johnny.

"Ted and I are looking at new homes and we're getting a bedroom for Johnny."

His own bedroom in a new home?! We're talking LA real estate. An additional bedroom could easily run you $500,000 to a $1 million extra. Johnny was suddenly worth hundreds of thousands of dollars to them? Chelsea and Ted were delusional. What power did Johnny possess?

He was technically a grown man—and an employee of Ted's company—and he was being treated as if he were their seven-year-old son. In fact, one weekend Johnny casually mentioned that he was going with Ted and his son, Will, to San Francisco for a 49ers game. What? Johnny was now being included in father-son bonding trips? That was ballsy, but apparently Ted now loved Johnny like one of his own. We might as well have started calling him little Johnny Harbert.

"It was great," Johnny assured me upon his return from the game. "We stayed at the W Hotel and we all shared a room. Lots of fun."

Any hopes of me becoming Ted's programming muse were crushed when Johnny lumbered in to work one morning looking exhausted. "Why do you look like shit?" I asked.

"I was up late watching TV pilots and helping Ted decide which shows should be ordered to series," Johnny answered.

I lost my mind. Johnny had officially assumed the role I had been dreaming of, and he had far less experience in television. He was only an associate producer, yet he was now guiding Ted's decision on which new show would follow *Keeping Up with the Kardashians* on Sunday night. I was crushed.

I'd finally had enough and needed to speak my mind. This, after all, was not rational, to me or anyone else. Employees don't live with their bosses. Was I the only one who understood this? This is like airplanes not taxiing before takeoff; it just didn't happen.

"Chelsea, Johnny can't live with you."

"Why not?" she asked. "Why can't he be happy?"

Wow. That was a good question, one for which I didn't have an answer. He did seem content and at peace for the first time since I'd known him. I always sensed that Johnny longed for the family and connections he gave up when he moved from Kansas to California. I guess he'd found them in an eighth-floor condo in Marina del Rey, California, with a burgeoning TV star and her executive boyfriend. Who was I to deny him happiness?

After long talks with my wife and others, I came to accept the arrangement and understood that it made Johnny and Chelsea happy. I couldn't be convinced it made Ted happy, but he did whatever Chelsea said. I stopped asking about the progress of Johnny's apartment and assumed Chelsea was helping him cover his lease, after which he'd be free and clear to live with Chelsea and Ted wherever they ended up. He was now a full-fledged Handler-Harbert.

Six months after Johnny moved in with Chelsea and Ted, we gathered for Chelsea's thirty-third birthday party at a restaurant in Venice, California. I'd had plenty to drink, and after I insisted, to the woman's face, that one of the makeup ladies on the show was not thirty-four and had to be "at least forty," it was time for the obligatory toasts.

Ted was always so awkwardly effusive when it came to Chelsea, and he was no different this time. He gushed about what a great person she was and how she'd turned his life around. At one point in his speech he remarked that Chelsea, on the one hand, could be so wonderfully caring and giving while at the same time "She can be so conniving and mercilessly fuck with people. Where's Brad Wollack?"

Ted looked around for me, and I excitedly waved like an unsuspecting idiot. "Over here, Ted!"

"Brad," Ted continued, "Johnny Kansas has *never* lived with us. He has never even set foot inside our condo! He's not coming on vacation with us; we're not getting him a bedroom in a new home. You are one big idiot."

I was floored! For six months I had wrestled with my emotions. I was concerned for Johnny, wrought with jealousy, and tormented by the ridiculous amount of time and patience a landlord had been granted to repair a fucking leak.

Johnny was relieved. He no longer had to avoid me for fear of slipping up. He had resorted to having little to no conversation with me, knowing full well he couldn't keep the secret anymore. He had been pulled in two different directions: one, obeying Chelsea; and two, revealing the lie to me so I wouldn't think he was a total mooching pussy.

Ultimately, I think the lie took as much of a mental toll on Johnny as it did on me. He was terrified of Chelsea and obeyed her every command, but he couldn't stand the fact that I thought he was living off her with no care in the world. Chelsea should really be thankful that he didn't have another ulcer.

SEXUAL HARASSMENT

It was December 2007, and Chelsea had been asked to host a year-end special for E! A few of us writers—Tom, Sue, and I—had been hired to help write the show. To avoid any conflicts with the *Chelsea Lately* production schedule, the special was to be shot at our regular studio on a Saturday.

That morning, I awoke to find an e-mail from Gary Snoonian, our executive in charge of production. Gary handles all of the budgets for our show and takes care of any logistics, including human resource matters. Gary, a self-loathing man of Armenian descent, is only remotely approachable when smoking a cigar or talking about horse racing, but is otherwise a coldhearted prick. Like any stiff, unfeeling jackass, Gary drives a no-frills Mercury Sable and is all business, all the time. You just don't fuck with Gary and the constant frown he wears on his pudgy, goateed face.

The e-mail he sent to me was brief: "Brad, please stop by my office when you get into the studio this morning." There are only two reasons you're called into Gary's office: one, to be scolded; or two, to be scolded, fired, and then physically removed from the premises by security. It's weird that workplaces never tell you when someone's getting canned, and you just have to sit there and pretend nothing's wrong while a poor girl sobs uncontrollably, makeup streaming down her face, and throws shit from her cubicle into a cardboard box. I really wish they could give more of a warning. It's just so awkward for everyone.

While getting ready to head to the office, I racked my brain for any possible infraction on my part. Sure, I was always saying inappropriate things. The rule at *Chelsea Lately* is that it hasn't been a productive morning writers meeting if I haven't made a 9/11 or Holocaust joke (and I'm talking about the Jewish Holocaust, not the Armenian Holocaust—no reason to get on Gary's bad side).

As I drove in that morning, I continued to ponder what Gary could possibly want to meet with me about. Obsessive thoughts and concerns ran through my head. As soon as I arrived at the studio, I walked into Gary's office and he instructed me to have a seat.

111

He was calm, mild-mannered, and even showed concern for me, which made it that much worse.

"So, someone has filed a harassment suit against Comcast," Gary said.

My heart skipped a beat. What did a harassment suit against a major corporation have to do with me?

"More specifically, they've made the complaint against you."

Oh, that's what.

"Who did?" I asked.

"I can't legally say," he added. "Can you think of anything inappropriate you may have said to someone in this office?"

I was shocked. Immediately a flood of memories of the horrible, degrading, and malicious things I had muttered around the halls of *Chelsea Lately* for the past seven months came rushing back to me. Man, I'd been a major, chauvinistic prick so many times I couldn't believe it.

"Nope," I said, looking straight into Gary's dark, scary eyes. "Can't think of anything inappropriate that I've ever said, Gary."

Hell, yeah, I remembered everything, but I was not about to admit it . . . and certainly not to a Mercury-driving Armenian. I didn't know which side Gary was on. For all I knew, Comcast was paying him to try to trap me.

My stomach dropped and my eyes drifted to the crayon doodles strewn across Gary's wall that his daughters had drawn. The contrast between the innocence of those pictures and the severity of the moment wasn't lost on me. Neither was the realization that I, too, would someday have to hang on my office wall the shitty little drawings my kids made.

"Really, you can't think of anything you've ever said?"

"No," I insisted. After a moment of silence, I asked, "Was it Elvira?"

The lady I was referring to wasn't actually named Elvira, but it was the name we assigned to the security guard who'd just been fired from the show. She had these electric blue eyes, and when she spoke, it was with an indistinguishable accent. It was kind of faux-British, but not really. She wore the strangest, witch-like outfits, which made no sense since there was a uniform for security guards. She was fucking creepy. It had to have been her. She was clearly pissed about being let go and wanted retribution. And even though she and I rarely, if ever, spoke, I was loud, outgoing, and well known in the office. I was an easy target. "Blame that boisterous fire crotch." Everyone else did.

"I can't say, Brad. Listen, Ted is on his way in to talk with you. We'll reconvene when he gets here."

Shit, this was serious. It was Saturday and Ted, the CEO, was on his way in to dress me down personally? It had gotten that high up already? Immediately my entire career flashed before my eyes. This was it. My stupid mouth was going to cost Comcast millions of dollars to settle this suit, I would be fired, and the entire industry would turn its collective back on me.

What would I tell my parents? What would I tell my

fiancée? How would I earn a living? Did this go on some permanent record? Would I go to prison? I couldn't go to prison—I'm small, white, and, again, very rape-able.

After leaving Gary's office, I lumbered back toward my own office, where Tom and Sue were waiting.

"You're never going to believe this," I said as I walked in. "Someone is suing Comcast for harassment based on something I said."

Immediately they peppered me with questions. Who was suing? What had I said? How did I react when Gary told me? What was I going to do? I slinked down in my desk chair and stared off into the distance, pondering my fate.

"Well, let's finish writing this stuff," Sue suggested.

Had she not heard me when I said that Comcast was being sued by some unidentified loon because of something I'd said? If the tables had been reversed, I would have been a little more concerned with consoling my officemate than making another fucking Lindsay Lohan joke.

Sue clearly didn't understand the gravity of this situation. Soon all of the big Comcast executives in Philadelphia—these industry titans—would not only know who I was, but would despise me for costing them millions of dollars. I was toast. Fuck, I was also a Comcast cable subscriber. Would they raise my rates or, worse, drop ESPN from my cable lineup?

My anxiety was increasing as I kept replaying the conversation with Gary over and over in my head. That's what compulsives do—we continuously replay the same scenario

TP0664841 9-001
VALERO 3657
700 LIGHTHOUSE
MONTEREY   CA 93

DATE   11/03/12
TIME   3:37 PM
AUTH# 035483

VISA

PUMP PRODUCT PPG
02   UNLD $3.859

GALLONS FUEL TOTAL
11.795 $45.52

Store #3657
700 Lighthouse
Monterey CA

in our heads, hoping for an alternative resolution or perspective on the event. That's what compulsives do—we continuously replay the same scenario in our heads. That's what compulsives do—we continuously replay the same scenario in our heads. We wonder if there was anything we could have done differently. It never helps. We just end up wallowing in our dread. With that, the twitches came roaring back and I was soon making popping noises with my lips.

I called my fiancée for some consolation. "I don't know what I'm going to do if I get fired, Shannon, but we'll stick together." She didn't admit it, but I could hear the concern and panic in her voice. She was clearly wondering how she'd gotten engaged to such a perverted loose cannon.

After twenty minutes of sitting in shock, I was jarred to my senses by my office line ringing. It was Gary. "Come down to my office. Chelsea's here and we want to speak with you."

Oh shit. I hadn't even thought about Chelsea. A new terror was upon me. When Chelsea gets mad, she gets bright red and the veins in her neck flare up, kind of like mine when I have that certain twitch. She, too, looks like a Velociraptor . . . only redder and with huge breasts. She was clearly going to be pissed. I shuffled back down to Gary's office, all the while picturing Chelsea yelling, "I fucking told you. You just couldn't shut your mouth."

Gary was in his chair and Chelsea was in one of the two chairs on the opposite side of the desk. Before I could even sit down, Chelsea launched into me.

"What did you say, Brad?!"

Yep, there were those veins . . . and those breasts.

"I don't know, Chelsea. I haven't said anything you haven't heard. I think whoever this is is just crazy."

"You must've said something, Brad. These things don't just come out of nowhere."

"I mean, you know we say all kinds of things in the writers' room."

"Well, Ted is on his way down here," she assured me. "And he is not happy. You'd better start thinking. Never mind this is 'a Saturday and this is his swimming time. Think, Brad!" Chelsea screamed. "What did you say?"

I racked my brain. Again, a million things came to my mind, but I was not about to incriminate myself.

Then Chelsea launched into a barrage of ridiculous questions.

"Did you ever say that someone had a nice ass?"

"No," I insisted.

"Did you ever ask someone to lift their shirt and show you their breasts?"

"What? No!"

"Did you ever tell someone you masturbated thinking about them?"

"That's fucking gross, Chelsea. No!"

And then came the question to end all questions.

"Brad, did you ever say you wanted to rape someone?"

For a moment the world stood still. I had to repeat

Chelsea's question in my own head just to make sure I'd heard it correctly.

"What?!" My face became flushed. "No, I never said I wanted to *rape* someone, Chelsea!" The truth is, at one time or another, we've all said these things to each other.

"Even as a joke?" Gary added.

I whipped my head around. "No, Gary, not even as a joke," I said, even though I knew, for sure, that not only had I been threatened with rape, but I had also threatened a rape. We all threaten each other all the time. But I had never, nor would I ever have, gone up to someone and said, "Hey there, I want to rape you."

At this point, I was not sure how any answer I gave would help the situation. If, for some reason, I did admit to telling someone I wanted to rape them, what was Chelsea going to do about it? Probably not a whole hell of a lot. It was safer to deny everything, but I had second thoughts. *Maybe,* I thought, *I'll admit to one rape comment to make it more believable that I'm denying everything else.*

It was at that point that even Chelsea couldn't take it anymore. She clearly saw the torment I was going through and had a rare soft moment. She initially presumed—and rightfully so, given my history—that I would go apeshit and throw a childish tantrum and start telling everyone that they could "Fuck off and suck my big, long balls! You can't bring Brad Wollack down!" Instead, I succumbed to the severity of the situation. No ranting or raving, just quiet panic.

117

I was terrified and had just turned, if possible, a paler shade than I normally was, when I saw her face softening into a wide smile and she began cracking up. Within seconds, tears were flowing from her eyes.

I turned to Gary, who was also laughing. Tom and Sue, who had been waiting outside the office listening to the whole exchange, came in applauding. Chelsea was now pointing to one of Gary's shelves.

I was so caught up in the moment I hadn't even noticed the video camera with the blinking light resting on the bookshelf behind Gary. These assholes were taping the whole thing, hoping to show my complete mental breakdown on a future *Chelsea Lately* episode.

I had never experienced a greater wave of relief at seeing a video camera taping me. I realized this was all a prank. Gary pointed to the camera on the bookshelf as if he were the Armenian Ashton Kutcher and we were on *Punk'd*, but all I could manage to say was, "You fuckers. I saw my whole career flash before my eyes!"

The tape never made air. At least there was one real takeaway from that day: Grumpy Gary isn't a bad actor.

GUESS WHO'S COMING TO THE OFFICE

Chelsea has never, for the life of her, understood what my wife, Shannon, could possibly find attractive about me—a pasty, red-haired, nerdy Jew. Nonetheless, her disapproval

A *drunk* Heather McDonald and her husband, Peter; me; Ted; Sue Murphy; Chelsea;
and Johnny.

of our nuptials, strictly on an aesthetic basis, didn't stop
her from attending our wedding in June 2008.

It was a beautiful summer evening as I wed the love of
my life in Beverly Hills. At the end of the evening, Chelsea
approached me and handed over an envelope containing a
very generous check. She never said what we should use
the money for, but my best guess was that she probably
wanted us to put it toward adopting a child in hopes of
our avoiding procreation, thus altogether eliminating the

119

possibility of a child coming out looking like a mini version of me.

We, on the other hand, applied the whole thing to our lavish honeymoon. Shannon and I had planned a ten-day trip to the gorgeous seaside town of Positano, Italy, and the island of Santorini in Greece. We'd spared no expense, opting to stay at the nicest of hotels, eat the best of foods, and go on whatever excursion we desired.

Ten days with your new bride and away from work seems idyllic, but I think the honeymoon is really an old-fashioned phenomenon. I haven't cross-referenced this, because I hate research, but it obviously dates back to the days when couples didn't know each other at all and women were still virgins when they got married. Basically, honeymoons, in my mind, were created so newlyweds could get emotionally and physically acquainted with their life partner.

However, Shannon and I had been together for six-plus years. We had been living together for two years, already had a healthy sexual relationship, and knew everything there was to know about each other. Needless to say, no matter how exotic the locale or romantic the setting, after ten days alone, two people run out of things to do and shit to say.

We were so desperate for conversation with other people that we were siding up at restaurants with couples we would *never* have associated with back home. I'm talking uber-Jews from New York and elderly widows from Florida. We became so anxious and delusional that we were even exchanging phone numbers, as if we were actually going to visit these a-holes back at home.

I became so jaded at points in the vacation that I thought about checking my e-mail. Before we left for the trip, I had made a promise to myself and, most important, to Shannon, that I wouldn't check my work e-mail during our honeymoon. I was going to focus on her and total relaxation—that was it.

I made it through Italy okay, mostly because my fat face was too busy buried in a plate of pasta twenty-four hours a day to think about anything else, but by the final few days in Greece, I was bored. Sure, we were at a beautiful resort, but it was nothing but sunlight. I can't stand the sun; it gave me melanoma once, so now I avoid it at all costs. In fact, when we sat by the gorgeous, peaceful infinity pool overlooking the deep blue sea, all tranquility at the resort was rudely disrupted every twenty minutes by one of the pool boys coming over to our chaise lounge and rotating my umbrella—by physically scraping the base of it across the pool deck. This was done to ensure that not one ounce of my skin was ever exposed to the sun. The other guests would look over, I would nod and give an apologetic wave, and Shannon would scold me. It was, however, great service.

Even in total shade, there is only so much sitting out I can do. I get restless and fidgety. Yes, the view was spectacular and my wife was—and is—gorgeous, and it was such a special place...blah, blah, blah. But I was fucking bored. And that's when I made the fatal mistake of check-ing my work e-mail on my iPhone.

After a few insignificant e-mails—most of which were from Chelsea and included photos of coworkers in compro-mising positions—I saw a message from an E! network pub-licist, John, with the subject line: Time Magazine Shoot.

Our show had been on the air for roughly a year and Chelsea was starting to get some big-time press. Natu-rally I assumed that John's message was just an informa-tive e-mail about a Chelsea article and the accompanying photo shoot that would take place in our offices. Basically, these e-mails are code for "Stay the fuck out of the way."

Instead, this was what I read.

HEY ALL:
    THE PHOTOGRAPHER FROM *TIME* MAGAZINE WILL
BE AT YOUR OFFICE AT 11AM TO PHOTOGRAPH ALL OF
THE WRITERS. IF THERE ARE ANY PROBLEMS, LET ME
KNOW ASAP.
    BEST,
    JOHN

My heart dropped and my face turned pale. Yeah, I have a fuckin' problem...I wasn't going to be there! Shan-non saw my look of horror and asked what was wrong.

"They're doing a *Time* magazine photo shoot of all the *Chelsea Lately* writers."

"That's great. So why do you look like shit?"

"Because it's on Friday and we don't get back to the States until Sunday."

I don't think of myself as a vain person per se, but there are a few things I like, and "credit" is one of them. The thought of being left out of a story about the people "behind Chelsea" in an international publication was too much to bear. Other than Tom, I had been with Chelsea the longest out of all of them. I deserved to be there! Immediately my mind began racing, wondering how I would answer all of the nagging questions from family and friends. "Why aren't you in the big article about Chelsea's writers, Brad? Does she not like you? Are you really even a writer for her? Are you a liar? Can you still get me tickets to a taping of the show?"

For a moment, rationality prevailed. "Okay, Brad," I assured myself, "there's no way this is true. Technically, since we're not covered by the Writers Guild of America there is no way that E! would allow a whole story to run about 'writers' on their network. Plus, it's *Time* magazine. Why would they want to run a story about the writers on a stupid basic cable show? They haven't even run a story about Chelsea. Hell, the writers couldn't even get a story in *Highlights* magazine. Why would *Time* run one?"

I took a few deep breaths, allowed the pool boy to rotate my umbrella, and tried to relax. I couldn't.

I turned to Shannon. "If this is a joke, why would John Rizzotti have cc'd all of the big executives at E!? He can't be bothering all of them with pranks like this. Plus, I made it very clear before I left that I wasn't checking my

123

work e-mail, so if this is a prank, they wouldn't have sent it to my work e-mail. This has to be real!"

I immediately pounded out an e-mail to Chelsea and Tom.

CHELSEA & TOM:
   WHAT'S THE DEAL WITH THE TIME PHOTO SHOOT?
   THERE'S NO WAY THEY CAN SHOOT IT ANOTHER DAY?

Tom replied.

NOPE. SORRY. YOU'LL JUST BE LEFT OUT. WE'LL TRY
AND MAKE SURE THEY AT LEAST MENTION YOUR NAME
IN THE ARTICLE.

"Try and make sure"? What the hell? How dare they? I had worked my ass off for Chelsea and all I could get out of them was a "we'll try"?

All of my instincts told me that this was a lie, a total hoax. But my instincts had also once told me that Sugar Ray was a great band with staying power. So, clearly my instincts weren't always spot on.

I was obsessed. I couldn't believe this was happening. Suddenly I became the worst person in the world to be with.

"I want to go home. This honeymoon sucks. I knew it was too long. I told you," I said to Shannon as my pool umbrella was being rotated yet again.

Now Shannon was pissed, and for two very valid

reasons. One, the anxiety it was causing me was ruining her honeymoon—the operative word being *her.* Two, we were in paradise and I was now being a complete asshole.

I had to get to the bottom of it, but if it were a hoax, I knew Chelsea and Tom wouldn't crack that quickly. I had to go to another source. I went to the weakest, most guilt-ridden person I knew: Johnny Kansas. If I tugged on his heartstrings hard enough and played up how emotionally distraught I was, he'd break down and tell me it was all a lie.

> JOHNNY, YOU'RE THE ONLY PERSON I CAN TRUST.
> THIS IS RUINING MY ENTIRE HONEYMOON. IS THIS
> *TIME* MAGAZINE SHOOT REAL?

Little did I know, Chelsea was one step ahead of me. She had already descended upon Johnny, knowing full well that I would try to exploit his weakness in my quest for the truth. Like a terrorist holding an AK-47 to the blindfolded head of her hostage, Chelsea had forced Johnny to go along with it.

He responded: Yes.

Recognizing that he could be monitored, I waited a few minutes and wrote again.

> JOHNNY, THIS IS RUINING EVERYTHING. IT'S THE
> LAST DAY OF MY HONEYMOON AND SHANNON IS
> PISSED. PLEASE TELL ME THE TRUTH. I KNOW I CAN
> TRUST YOU. DON'T BETRAY THAT.

Johnny's an easy one to break. All you have to do is question his trust and loyalty, and he instantly squawks. But this time there was no immediate response, only radio silence. My heart sank, my head swelled, and my twitches ignited. I waited five minutes and checked again. Nothing. Beads of sweat, entirely unrelated to the heat, began to form. I was not sure what was happening to me physically, but I could only imagine that this was the beginning of a severe anxiety attack. And on a tranquil pool deck in Greece was not where I wanted to lose my shit. I had to do something.

"That's it, we're heading home early," I announced. Shannon freaked, but I told her that she and I had, in theory, a lifetime together but "This may be my only shot for *Time* magazine." As she continued to yell at me, I snapped, "Fine, you can stay here and I'll head home early." This marriage was clearly getting off on the right foot.

I hustled my ass up to the hotel's business center, plopped down at a desk, and used the phone to call the airline. We had originally booked first class, but the only available seats were in economy, and the fee to downgrade was almost a thousand dollars—not to mention our having to forfeit the final night at the hotel, for which we'd already paid. "Fuck it," I said. "Advertisers pay millions to be in *Time* magazine. I can afford to pay eighteen hundred dollars to be in *Time*."

The tickets home were changed—Shannon was coming

126

back early with me whether she liked it or not. And she was definitely not going to like it...especially since we were now both in economy—and I put her in the middle seat. Hell, I was hating the thought of travelling sixteen hours in coach, too, but I was focusing on the greater good: a *Time* magazine photo spread.

Having made the change, I felt better but understood that this was not the ideal way to end a honeymoon. From champagne to shit. I was still not sure how to tell Shannon that we needed to go pack up immediately. So I didn't. When I returned to the pool, I pussyfooted around the issue, telling her that I'd "looked into changing the tickets, but didn't actually make the change." Even "looking into" got me in trouble.

She was pissed off and started crying. She couldn't believe that I would even consider going back early. I began to realize I would be in deep shit when it came time to tell her that I hadn't just "considered" it; we *were* going home early. At that moment, I fully accepted that I might have to resort to drugging her and dragging her ass to the airport.

"They're just fucking with you and you're stupid enough to fall for it!" she yelled before storming off.

I yelled after her, "But what if they're not?! I have to be in *Time* magazine, Shannon!" I decided to hang back a bit and let her cool off. At least I hoped she was going to cool off.

Needless to say, the pool boys hadn't been by to rotate my umbrella recently—they wanted no part of our marital problems. I got up and glared at the nearest pool boy as I struggled to rotate the umbrella myself. Then I slinked back down into the deck chair and checked my e-mail again. There was a message from Johnny.

Too timid to defy Chelsea outright, he responded to my last pleading e-mail as best he could without actually revealing anything. But like death row inmates sending coded messages, I understood the subtext of his e-mail.

BRAD, THERE IS NO REASON TO LET THIS RUIN YOUR
. HONEYMOON.

Oh shit. Just then I realized that the whole thing had been a lie—an awful, tumultuous Chelsea Handler lie that had sought to drive me crazy and disrupt my blissful, once-in-a-lifetime (I think) honeymoon. I was now out $1,800, my wife was pissed at me, and worst of all, there would be no *Time* magazine shoot.

How would I reveal this to Shannon? She'd been right and I'd been wrong. Not only would I pay the immediate consequences, but for the rest of our marriage I knew that she would lord this over me, never missing the chance to remind me who was right and who was dead wrong.

It was going to be bad enough when I told her that it was all a lie. I couldn't top it off with "Oh, and we are actually going home a day early...and we're in economy...

and it cost us eighteen hundred dollars." It would have been too traumatic for her. And she would have wasted no time insisting that, as punishment, I buy her an eighteen-hundred-dollar Chloe purse. Somehow my losing money means I always have to spend the equivalent on her. I've never been certain of her logic there.

I returned to the business center to change our flights back to the original itinerary. Good news: we could switch back for a very slight fee. Bad news: there was only one seat left in first class. Relieved just to be back on the initial flight, I accepted and decided to worry later about explaining to Shannon why she was flying economy and I was still in first.

With the matter resolved and our love restored, Shannon and I wrapped up the honeymoon as intended.

Checking in at the airport on the day of our departure, we received our boarding passes and Shannon wondered why we weren't sitting together. Still attempting to cover my tracks, I stupidly decided to sternly ask the ticket agent, "Sir, why are we *both* not sitting in first class as our itinerary states? There has to be an error."

Not appreciating my tone, the all-business ticket agent wasted no time in looking at the monitor and explaining ever so bluntly, "Because our records show that you changed your flight, and when you changed it back there was only one first-class seat remaining." He looked at Shannon and said, "Your husband bought you a ticket in coach, Mrs. Wollack. Enjoy your long flight and enjoy your marriage to him."

Shannon glared at me. The jig was up. I offered a sheep-ish grin, and she simply said, "You're an idiot." Then she took my first-class ticket and handed me hers. That's why I married her: she knows me so well.

As Shannon settled into her plush first-class seat with a mimosa, I lumbered back to the forty-eighth row of the plane, climbed over two smelly Greeks, and assumed my seat in the dead center seat of the middle row. Even worse? The smelly Greek to my left was reading—wait for it—*Time* magazine. Clearly that was someone's way of saying, "In your face, asshole."

While I forgave Chelsea soon after, Shannon did not forgive as easily. My first day back at the office, I received the following e-mail from her.

TELL THEM THAT WE WANT THE $1,000 BACK FROM THE NIGHT/DAY THEY RUINED AT ONE OF THE BEST HOTELS IN THE WORLD. I COULD BUY A NEW PURSE WITH THAT MONEY.

Considering that Chelsea had helped fund half the trip with her wedding gift, I wasn't going to ask her to pay us back, but I did appreciate that Shannon, my won-derful new bride, clearly had her purse-buying priorities straight.

Chelsea Handler has caused me extreme turmoil, angst, fear, and thousands of dollars in psychiatry bills that aren't

My dad, Chelsea, and me in Tahoe. You can see Chelsea's enthusiasm in hanging out with my family.

covered by my insurance. However, in the end, I've realized what this all means: if Chelsea takes the time and energy out of her insanely hectic life and goes to extraordinary lengths to screw yours up royally, leaving you utterly humiliated and degraded, then you'll know you're good to go. She clearly loves you.

Chelsea, for everything you've done, thank you and . . . fuck off.

———

I want to go on record that Shannon is a very close friend of mine, and I would never have allowed Brad to return from their honeymoon early. I would have come clean had I known that Brad was egomaniacal enough to shortchange his bride on her honeymoon for a picture in a magazine. He is a sad, sad clown. My apologies to Shannon exclusively.

—Chelsea

Shannon and Chelsea in Turks and Caicos without me. Chelsea says she prefers not to see my body on her vacations.

Chapter Six

Dial Tone, a Chelsea Specialty

AMBER MAZZOLA

C helsea Handler is a dirty fucking liar. But what most people don't know is she respects honesty and loyalty

Chelsea and me in London on her very first book tour.

more than anything. That is, if it's on her terms. But she's okay with lying if it's for a joke because for her, laughter trumps all.

My friendship with Chelsea started ten years ago, when she was one of the stars of the hidden camera show *Girls Behaving Badly*. She would offer happy endings at car washes, sit in shopping carts yelling at passersby, drink vodka and sodas at bars while wearing a pregnancy suit, and test out makeup artists for her "newborn," to name a few stunts. I was the girl who jumped out of a cardboard box, camera in hand, in the middle of Ventura Boulevard, screaming, "You've just been pranked by *Girls Behaving Badly*!" We were quite a pair.

Back then, Chelsea was paid to lie. Now she does it as a hobby.

"Sarah" is the pseudonym Chelsea gave me in her three books. The anonymity was a nice touch, until she decided to blow my cover on Jay Leno when she referred to her friend Amber who took off her shirt in the London restaurant Dining in the Dark. Immediately after, I got dozens of text messages from people I hadn't heard from in years, people I wasn't that interested in hearing from.

"That was *you*? Did you *really* take your top off at a restaurant?"

Everyone knows Chelsea is a liar, so I just chalked it up to that. "Oh, come on! Do you really think I would take my top off? Of course not!" Chelsea's reputation comes in handy.

Sometimes, very rarely, she lies for the right reasons, if that's at all possible.

When I was going through a horrible breakup that would make most women curl into a ball and never leave the house, Chelsea had a rough time.

"It's okay, Chelsea," I would say to console her, handing her a tissue. "Everything happens for a reason."

"I know. It just sucks," she would say in between crocodile tears.

"I know. I know it does."

This was *my* breakup, but for some reason, Chelsea was taking it way worse than I was. One night, while we were at her aunt and uncle's house in Bel Air drinking vodka and eating more than a pound of Costco-size brie, the usual Sunday staple at the Burkes', a hot guy came over to pick up Chelsea. Chelsea got a little weird and tried to hurry the guy out of there, saying he was her accountant and she had to go do her taxes.

I didn't question the tax session with a hot guy on a Sunday evening in July. Why would I have? Who would lie about doing taxes? As soon as Chelsea left, her aunt informed me that the guy was a date, someone Chelsea had met on Myspace (yes, Myspace) and didn't want to tell me about because she thought it would hurt my feelings, what with my breakup. Truth is, Chelsea needed this rebound to get over my ex more than I did. I had been encouraging her to start dating again for weeks.

At 2:00 AM, Chelsea came over to my dad's house (I

had moved in with him after the breakup) and crawled into bed with me, to make sure I didn't spend the night alone or wake up alone. She was very persistent about this, and for months she had slept in my childhood room, in my canopy bed draped in Paper White linens, with my glow in the dark solar system overhead and the Laura Ashley flower-print border wrapped around the room.

One morning, I woke up to sunlight pouring in through my bedroom window, heating up the room like a sauna. Chelsea was lying above the sheets buck naked except for her underwear. Her tank top, which had started the evening on her body, was tied around her eyes like a bandana to shield her from the light.

"Um . . . ?" I couldn't help but laugh. She looked ridiculous.

"Fuck off. It's ninety degrees in here! How can you sleep like this?" Chelsea asked.

"I dunno. I'm used to it."

"Well, you're going to have to start sleeping at my place."

My seventy-five-year-old father is always freezing. In ninety-degree weather, he sports a long-sleeve shirt and pants. There's no way he'd let me sleep with the air on. I tried it once. The minute he heard it, he shut it off immediately.

That night, I started sleeping at Chelsea's apartment, which was a whole different experience. Air-conditioning on full blast, curtains as dark as a hotel room in Vegas, and eye shades. Regardless, the company was nice, and Chelsea was right—it would have sucked to go to bed and wake up alone. While promoting her first book, *My Horizontal Life,* she flew from Los Angeles to Las Vegas to San Francisco and then back to Los Angeles all in one day just to make sure I wasn't alone.

I think what got me through the breakup was the fact that I had to be strong—for Chelsea. This brief period may have been the only time in our friendship when Chelsea didn't fuck with me. But the moment she heard me talking about other boys and dating again, she was back at it.

Let me explain something before you think I'm just another one of those gullible idiots duped by Chelsea. As an only child, I didn't grow up playing practical jokes on siblings. My biggest lies involved why I was late for curfew. I am an amateur; Chelsea is a professional. And what makes her so good is not only her commitment to the lie, but a deadly combination of speed and creativity. When you're grilling her for the truth, she has already thought of the next answer before you even have the question. Plenty of times I've smelled such an answer coming from a mile away and called her out for being full of shit, but there has been a time or two when I've fallen prey to one of her lies.

I was on the phone with my psychic one morning when Chelsea called on the other line. I didn't want to click over to her because I was getting good info on my love life, but Chelsea was relentless. She kept calling until I picked up.

"What's your game plan?" she asked.

"I'm on the phone with Sydney."

"You're an asshole."

"Whatever. It's not like you don't call her."

"Not every day. You have to stop taking advantage, Amber," she said.

Chelsea and I have known Sydney for years. We have each driven over sixty miles outside of Los Angeles to see her, for the sole purpose of pumping her for information about our lives—as if she weren't onto us. She knew exactly what we were doing. But I think she enjoyed our company as much as we enjoyed the brain-picking sessions.

In fact, one day Chelsea even endured an hour-long lecture on birds from Sydney's boyfriend, who is a falconer, just to get a kernel of information from Sydney. Who's the asshole now?

Sydney once told Chelsea she would have a talk show one day, way before she had one. Chelsea didn't believe her. Back then, she had no desire for a talk show. So, regardless of how Chelsea likes to poke fun at my friendship with Sydney, she's still a true believer.

"See if Sydney tells you that I hooked up with P. Diddy last night," Chelsea said.

"Oh, my God, did you really?"

"Call me when you're done."

"Wait, are you really sleeping with P. Diddy?"

This is a recurring problem with Chelsea. You can't believe a word she says. She's the girl who cried wolf.

"Hello?"

There was a dial tone, a Chelsea specialty. When she is done talking, she hangs up mid-sentence. This isn't reserved for phone conversations, either. It is Chelsea's MO for all forms of contact. When she is done with whatever it may be—a party, a date with a guy, dinner with a friend, a phone call—she'll abort. She's not very good with good-byes.

I called Chelsea back to pump her for the P. Diddy info, but she wasn't biting. She just said, "This is going to be an interesting fall..." Then, clearly changing the subject: "What are you and the Persian doing for New Year's?"

"I don't know. I haven't thought about it."

The Persian she was talking about was my fiancé, Zoughi. She's never called him by name. I know, you're probably thinking, *Fiancé? Weren't you just breaking up with someone?* I don't mess around.

"A bunch of us are going to the Bahamas for New Year's," Chelsea said. You guys should come."

I have been all over the world with Chelsea—Australia, London, Mexico, Turks and Caicos. And the vacations have a lot in common: a beach, a boat ride, lots of Belvedere, late night dance parties, and chicken fingers at 4:00 AM. They're really the perfect getaways. So I've always welcomed another Chelsea adventure, and at that point in my life, the Bahamas sounded great.

I think I was more excited about this trip because it would be my first with Chelsea and Zoughi, and Chelsea was finally accepting that I was in a relationship with the

"Persian" and not her brother Roy, whom she had been trying to set me up with since their mother's funeral. Literally, *at* the funeral. In fact, Chelsea continued to try to hook me up with Roy well into my engagement and at my bachelorette party. It got a little awkward a couple of times. But that might have been because I always did have a little crush on Roy. He's the sarcastic, witty, loyal male version of Chelsea. What's not to like?

Bahamas prep began. I waxed all the hair off my body. I tried to wax Zoughi's back, so Chelsea wouldn't take pictures of him and show them on national TV or Twitter, but no such luck. Ever since Zoughi had heard what a pansy my ex-fiancé was, he overexerted himself to be the polar opposite of him in every way. And this included the area of hair removal.

After an eighteen-hour travel day, Zoughi and I finally arrived at The Cove to find the usual suspects in the usual position: poolside with margaritas.

"Hi, Zoughi!" Chelsea yelled. "Hi, Amber!"

We approached the pool, said hello to friends, and met a few newbies to the group. There was always a newbie or two. Chelsea's philosophy has always been "the more the merrier." She gets bored with us at times and likes to spice up vacations with fresh meat she can prey on.

"Zoughi, meet Navid. He's a fellow Persian like you," Chelsea said.

Phew! Now it won't be Zoughi getting the brunt of all the Persian jokes, I thought. And there would be someone in

The day I got to the Bahamas.

our party with a hairier back then Zoughi. I gave Chelsea a lot of credit. Two Persians on one vacation, in one pool. She must have been feeling charitable. I do find it funny, though, that Chelsea would make such fun of Persians when she dated one for quite a while.

"Jesus, Amber, put some fucking lotion on your feet," Chelsea said.

"Take it easy. I just got here."

Before I knew it, she was out of the pool, grabbing her Bath and Body Works lotion, and attacking my feet, rubbing lotion all over my toes, in my nail bed, up my leg. Lots of it. Two coats. I'm not going to lie: it felt good. Would you come all lubed up if you knew you were going to get a rubdown every time Chelsea saw you? I'm no dummy.

"It's just dry skin," I said. "I've been traveling for hours."

"It's disgusting. You should be ashamed of yourself." Then she grabbed my hands and lathered them up as well.

My dry skin is the one thing about me that drives Chelsea crazy. Well, that and the fact that I'm always late to everything and she's always early and waiting on me.

Our first night in the Bahamas we had sushi for dinner, because why should we do anything different from what we do every night in Los Angeles? Everyone was pretty tired from traveling. Everyone but Chelsea, who tried to keep the party going. Zoughi and I wanted to go to bed. We hadn't unpacked, which is what I like to do first when I arrive someplace new, and we had been awake for over twenty-four hours. Knowing Chelsea wouldn't take well to the "I'm tired" excuse, I decided to try her tactic: the Irish good-bye. I would feign interest just until I had enough, then I would abruptly leave without telling anyone and without explaining myself to anyone. Seemed simple enough. It worked like a charm for Chelsea.

Once we finished dinner, we walked out to the casino, where Chelsea and the gang wanted to play blackjack. Zoughi and I proceeded to the tables with everyone, and when we realized there was no room to sit at the blackjack table that Chelsea had chosen, we headed straight for the

Chelsea and me at Nobu that night.

elevators. No one saw us. No one cared. It was a perfectly executed plan.

Right when I put that keycard in the door to our room, however, I got a text from Chelsea.

"Where are you?" she asked.

"In my room." I decided to try the honest approach first.

"Why?"

"My feet hurt. Changing shoes." And that's where *my* lie started.

"Hurry back down," she replied. "A seat opened up next to me."

"Okay."

I didn't make a move. Then, twenty minutes later, I got another text.

"Are you down here?" Chelsea asked.

I'm not sure what possessed me to pull a Chelsea, but my lie continued to escalate. "Yeah, I'm playing blackjack."

"Where?"

"On the other side of the casino."

"Come to us."

"I couldn't find you. And I found a lucky table."

"Okay. We'll come to you."

Shit, now what? "Can't text. Pit boss just yelled at me."

No response.

I'm sure she knew I was full of shit when I decided to make the pit boss a part of my lie. What was I thinking? I don't pay attention if a flight attendant, a cop, or Oprah says, "No cell phones," so I would never listen to a pit boss in the Bahamas. Chelsea knew this. Her silent treatment meant she knew I was still up in my room.

"Crap. Chelsea knows I'm lying," I said to Zoughi.

"She doesn't care," Zoughi assured me. "Everyone else is there with her."

So, instead of going out, I did the one thing I'd wanted to do since I got to the Bahamas: unpack. Once my OCD was satiated and everything was neatly folded in drawers, I crawled under the fluffy comforter to go to bed. This was probably the only night I was going to go to bed sober, so I planned to take full advantage.

The next morning, I woke to my phone ringing. I figured Chelsea was calling to give me shit for ducking out early last night. Or she wanted to work out. Neither sounded appealing.

"What are you doing?" she asked.

"Nothing. I just woke up."

"The hotel is being evacuated. You have to pack up your stuff."

"Oh, shit. Really? Why?"

"There's a flood."

"Where's it coming from?"

"I don't know. I'm not a plumber. Don't you see water seeping through?"

I looked around our room and up at the ceiling. "No."

"Well, you're lucky. It's all over my bathroom. And Roy's bedroom is flooded. The water ruined his phone."

I looked out the window. People were carrying about their business, and no one seemed in a hurry. "People outside are going to the pool, though."

"Amber, stop fucking around! The concierge says we have twenty-six minutes until we're swimming out of here! Get to the boat. I've got to finish packing." She yelled out, "Rico, you can take that one bag by the door."

Click. Dial tone. And away she went.

Shit. "Zoughi, we need to pack everything back up. We're being evacuated."

"Huh?" He looked out the window. "Why?"

"There's a flood in the hotel."

145

I took my suitcase and feverishly began to stuff it with all my clothes and crap. This was so annoying, since just eight hours prior, I had unpacked everything so nice and neatly.

Zoughi couldn't have cared less about packing anything but his iPad.

We gathered our stuff and booked it out of the room. Because of my fear of taking an elevator in an emergency, we proceeded to the stairs. Thanks to Chelsea, we'd gotten a penthouse, and now thanks to Chelsea, we had to walk down sixteen flights of stairs with our oversize luggage in tow.

My bags clanked down each step, but there was no way I was going to lift seventy pounds. By the time we got to the bottom, we were soaked in sweat and out of breath. Unfortunately for us, we still had to get to the marina, on the other side of the property. Outside, everything still looked calm, though the hotel did seem more desolate than yesterday. I wondered where the water was coming from.

When we got on the boat, everyone was talking about the flood. Most had actually seen water seeping through the ceiling of their rooms. I looked around as everyone was talking and I noticed that Zoughi and I were the only ones with luggage.

"Where's all your stuff?" I asked Chelsea.

"It's being shipped."

"What about yours?" I asked Ivory.

"Front desk has it."

"So what happens when the lobby floods?"

"They'll ship it!" Chelsea snapped.

I noticed that Chelsea had her arm in a sling. "What happened to you?" I asked, pointing at her arm.

"I slipped."

"On water? It was that bad?"

"Don't you ever listen? It was really bad in my room. I slipped and landed on my arm. The hotel nurse said it's sprained."

Chelsea walked off to the front of the boat, holding onto her arm. I felt bad for her. What a crappy way to spend the rest of your beach vacation.

"Where are we gonna stay?" I asked Ivory. "Do we have another hotel?"

"Chelsea's checking into it now."

Just as I said that, Chelsea came back over with the captain in tow.

"Hey, the captain says we've exceeded the weight limit on the boat. You have to get rid of some things in your bags."

"You're joking, right?"

Chelsea looked up toward the captain for support.

"No, ma'am."

I couldn't believe this. Were our clothes really going to make a difference with all the weight on the boat? Sounded like we needed to eliminate a person or two. But I didn't want to make a scene, so I quietly kneeled down and unzipped my first bag. Chelsea took my other suitcase and started to pull stuff out by the handful. My heart raced a little faster as I saw all my hard folding work go down the tubes.

"These have got to go!" she said as she picked up a pair of flip-flops.

"What? They weigh nothing!"

"Well, something's gotta go."

I was becoming increasingly agitated as I took more stuff out of my bag: shoes, makeup, bathing suits, every charger known to man. There was a heaping pile growing higher and higher next to my suitcase. "What the hell do I do with all this?"

When I turned around to look at Chelsea, she was laughing uncontrollably. She was bright red and could barely breathe. "Throw it overboard" she said, holding her coslopus for dear life.

"I'm glad you think this is funny!"

I was so annoyed. I looked over at Ivory, who was also laughing. Was this all a big joke? "No way. Are you guys fucking serious?"

Laughter started to erupt around the boat. Everyone was laughing at me, including the captain.

"You guys suck!" I looked toward Hannah. "You too?"

She nodded her head, laughing with the rest of them.

I couldn't believe it. Were Zoughi and I the only ones told this lie? The entire boat knew? Even the captain? And the Persian with the hairier back than Zoughi's? That was just so embarrassing.

How had I let it get so far? It wasn't like I couldn't take a joke. I could. But I felt stupid and I hated feeling stupid. I silently refolded my clothes, pissed.

So there I sat for the entire boat trip with two oversize pieces of luggage by my side. Anytime someone walked by, they smirked. Needless to say, Chelsea's arm was no longer in a sling. She snapped a picture of me flanked by the two large suitcases. Instantly it was up on Twitter. I figured there was no getting out of that one.

Just then, I couldn't help myself. I started to laugh as well. This really was a ridiculous situation. Plus, it's hard for me to stay mad at Chelsea. I'm the idiot who'd believed her.

There was no time to be angry. The boat had anchored at a sandbar near Norman's Cay, and everyone was jumping off the boat and swimming in the crystal blue waters, having fun. I wanted in on that action. Good thing I had my suitcase and ample bathing suit options.

When we got back to the hotel, which was not submerged underwater, we all went to the casino. I was not going to risk leaving early this time and be the asshole again.

Going to a casino with Chelsea is a unique experience. The vodka is flowing and so are the chips. Luckily, I was playing with Chelsea's chips and not my own. We planted ourselves at one blackjack table, right next to a loud-mouthed Israeli and his four equally annoying sons, who were betting five-hundred-dollar hands. The father was flirting with Chelsea hard core and had no idea who she was. But his four kids knew, and they were mortified by their dad. A situation like this really highlights one of the many differences between Chelsea and the rest of us. Most of us, when confronted with a drunk Israeli at a blackjack table, will either ignore him or ask to be left alone, but not Chelsea. Chelsea engages. An hour at that table and she knew everything there was to know about this guy, and he knew nothing truthful about her.

As the night wore on, she grew tired of her games with the Israeli and was ready to be done gambling. This meant going "all in," because to her, exchanging chips back to cash is a hassle. She looked up at the dealer, pushed all her chips toward him, and said, "Take this. I want to go to my room." He politely got blackjack and took them all away.

At 4:00 AM, we continued the party up in Chelsea's room. The other Persian whipped out a box of cigarettes, which looked appealing to everyone in our shitfaced condition. But no one had a lighter. Chelsea promptly called room service to solve the problem.

"Hi, this is Chel-say-ya," she enunciated slowly. For whatever reason, Chelsea has a tendency to disguise her voice when she calls room service. "Can you please bring up some matches?" she asked.

We were in a nonsmoking hotel, so the person on the other line was clearly suspicious.

"I don't want to smoke," Chelsea assured the person, with the phone in one hand and a cigarette in the other. "I'd like to take a bath and light some candles."

The person on the other end wasn't falling for it.

"Okay, fine. I need to get some matches for my book club that's about to start," she said.

The whole room was laughing.

"Yes, we're about to start *From Pieces to Weight,* a 50 Cent thriller, and I need to get in the right mood."

I could hear the response on the other end of the phone: "I'm sorry, Miss Handler."

"Fine. I'll take chicken fingers."

Room service came shortly thereafter. There were no matches.

By almost 5:30 AM, the party had started to unwind and Chelsea had retreated to her bedroom after a chicken finger, so I thought it was safe to leave. After all, Chelsea was harmless when she was sleeping. Plus we had a car picking us up in a couple hours to take us to the airport.

The trip back was another long day of traveling. I kept thinking about the poor fools back at the hotel who would fall prey to Chelsea's voodoo. All in all, Zoughi and I made it through the trip relatively unscathed.

When we walked in the door to our apartment, there were about a dozen flower arrangements scattered throughout the living room. I had no idea what they were for.

I started to read the cards: "Congrats you guys!" "So happy for you." "You deserve it."

Most of them were from family members and close friends, so I figured they were for our engagement—until I came across a card that read, "Can't wait to be an auntie!"

"Auntie? Maybe these are for the wrong apartment."

The doorbell rang. Another delivery.

"Hi, this is for a Zoo-wa—"

"Zoughi," I interjected.

"Yeah, can you sign here?"

This one read, "Zoughi, hope you feel better. Let me know if you need anything."

I didn't get it. Sympathy and congratulations?

I turned on my BlackBerry, and text messages started pouring in. Clearly I had to Sherlock Holmes this situation. There was a series of texts from Zoughi's brother, Farshad. I called him.

"Oh, my God," he said upon hearing my voice. "Are you okay? How are you feeling? How's my brother doing?"

"Good, we just got home."

"Cool. Have you told anyone in the family yet?"

"No, we literally just got in. Feel free to spread the word."

"Does my brother know?"

"Know what?"

"About the e-mail you sent earlier."

Farshad then forwarded me an e-mail that I had supposedly written to my soon-to-be brother-in-law. It read:

I JUST TOOK A PREGNANCY TEST. I'M PREGNANT AND
I'M NOT KIDDING. I'M ON MY WAY HOME.

Just then, it all made sense. Chelsea was continuing to fuck with me. From three thousand miles away. Impressive.

"Oh, my god, Zoughi, where is my iPad?"

"I don't know. You packed it."

I texted Chelsea. "Hey, did I leave my iPad there?"

No response for a few minutes. Then: "You're a hot mess."

And there was my answer. I had left my iPad in Chelsea's room in the Bahamas and she had randomly e-mailed a bunch of people from my address book. Since Chelsea is electronically challenged, I was surprised she'd figured out how to use the iPad to begin with.

She'd created a real shit storm in my conservative, Catholic family, who now thought the reason I was getting married was because I was pregnant. For weeks everyone was talking about my shotgun wedding and how I needed to buy a new wedding dress that would flatter a pregnant belly. This, of course, was hilarious to Chelsea.

It wasn't until everyone came back from the Bahamas that the sympathy cards for Zoughi started to make sense as well.

When I was at dinner with Ivory one night, she asked, "So how's Zoughi doing?"

"He's good. Back to work."

"Well, that's good. Does he need surgery?"

"For what?"

"His knee!"

Ivory could see by the look on my face that I had no idea what she was talking about. "Chelsea told us what happened," she said, giggling.

"Well, why don't you tell *me* what happened, since apparently I have no idea what you're talking about."

"Chelsea said that when he fell, he busted his knee."

"He didn't fall!"

"She said that night you left early, you and Zoughi had taken peyote and you guys were rolling—"

"Peyote?"

"Yeah. I thought it was weird, but she said there had been a resurgence in Middle Easterners using peyote."

"Uh-huh." I couldn't wait to hear what line of bullshit was coming next.

"And that you guys had crazy sex and Zoughi fell off the bed and broke his knee."

"From the peyote?"

"Yeah, I guess."

"Ivory, peyote is for Native American Indians. Zoughi is fucking Persian. How do you think we would even get peyote in the Bahamas?"

"She said that Zoughi always travels with it. Like a ritual. Oh, my God, I can't believe I am so stupid. What is wrong with all of us? Chelsea begged me not to tell you that I knew about the peyote."

"And what else?" I asked her.

"And the reason you left early was because Zoughi had to be airlifted back to the mainland and then taken immediately to an American hospital because of his insurance or something. I guess he's with an HMO?"

I just sat there staring at Ivory.

"None of this is true, is it?" she asked.

"No! We came back early to make it in time for Tanya's New Year's Eve party!"

"So Zoughi's knee is fine?"

"Yes, his knee is fine. It's like we're dealing with a seven-year-old with Chelsea."

"A seven-year-old with really big tits and a lot of money," Ivory reminded me.

"This is true."

Unbelievable. Chelsea had used my e-mail to screw me and my fiancé in our circle of friends and family. Now I had to put out a lot of fires: convince my family that I wasn't pregnant and that my marriage to Zoughi was not a shotgun wedding. And to top it off, I had to convince my friends that I didn't have a drug problem or kinky sex issues and that Zoughi's knee was just fine. Zoughi, however, thought the knee thing was funny and started limping when we were out with friends. Of course, Chelsea turned the limp into a prosthetic leg in her book *Chelsea Chelsea Bang Bang*.

I called Chelsea later to tell her I knew about everything. "Nice work," I said.

"You are so dumb," she said, before hanging up on me.

Actually I was smart enough to realize one thing. If Chelsea doesn't fuck with you, she doesn't care. And it's easy to see why I keep coming back for more. She's spontaneous and compassionate. She favors individuality. She roots for the underdog, and her loyalty never wavers, not even for the sake of a joke. She is truly a friend.

155

But I'll tell you this. If that bitch ever learns how to use Facebook, we are all fucked!

I would like to go on the record and say that Amber is currently pregnant, so in essence, anything I was "lying" about was simply me telling the future. As with many psychics, my facts are right but my timing can be off.

As far as Zoughi's knee injury goes, there is still time for that.

Love,
Chelsea

Chelsea and me at my real wedding.

Chapter Seven

Go Lakers

JOSH WOLF

The one thing that has been consistent about Chelsea Handler since the day I met her is that she is painfully honest. She will tell you the truth, even if you don't want to hear it, anytime she feels it needs to be said.

At the same time, you can't believe a fucking word she says.

Crazy combo, right? She is one of the truest, most loyal friends you could ever hope to have in your lifetime, but if the window is cracked open even a bit for her to fuck with you, she will say and make you believe anything so she can have a good laugh.

That's harder to handle than you would think. Luckily, I was prepared. I grew up with three older brothers who waged mental warfare on me for my entire childhood. They had me convinced for years that I was adopted but that my parents would never admit it because they didn't want to hurt my feelings. They said that if I talked to our parents about it, my mom would most likely kill herself.

Not wanting to be responsible for my mom's untimely demise, I resisted the temptation.

After a while, I suspected they were lying. There were pictures of me all over the house, and my brothers and I kind of looked the same, but every time my mom or dad yelled at me, my oldest brother would be sure to tell me that they were harder on me because "I wasn't blood." It wasn't until I heard my grandmother talking about how she was at the house when my parents brought me home from the hospital that I was able to put the final pieces of the puzzle together.

"I knew it! I knew I wasn't adopted!" I shot up and screamed. Everybody just stared at me. They had no fucking idea what I was talking about. Shit, my brother barely remembered. He hadn't teased me about it in years. I was eleven years old. Since then, I have learned to take everything anyone says with a grain of salt. Especially assholes like Chelsea Handler.

My wife does not.

My wife, Beth, is an extremely intelligent woman. She's a writer and director whose films have won awards all over the world. She also might be the single nicest person on the face of the earth, someone who always comes from a place of truth and who takes what people say at face value because that's how she treats people in return. Unfortunately, all of those amazing traits also make her very susceptible to practical jokes.

How did she end up with an asshole like me? No idea.

My wife, Beth, and Chelsea in NYC.

Sometimes I feel bad bringing her around my jerk-off friends because we are all such assholes. Our idea of fun is hurling insults at one another and pulling pranks that have a good possibility to humiliate. So when I started bringing her around Chelsea and the gang, I thought, *This might get ugly.*

Things were fine for a while, until one day when we were all hanging out at Chelsea's and somebody brought up the Lakers. As soon as Chelsea heard the word *Lakers,* she said, "Oh yeah, I just won fifty thousand dollars on that game last night." This is her thing. Whenever someone brings up a sports team, she talks about how much money she won on a game they played in. Every single time.

My wife then said, "Fifty thousand dollars? Oh my god, Chelsea. That's amazing."

And that's when Chelsea smelled blood.

Let me say, first of all, that Chelsea Handler does not know one thing about sports. Totally retarded. Wait, I take that back, she knows *one* thing: the 1986 New York Mets. And I have to admit, she's kind of a genius the way she uses them. Since it's the only sports team she knows anything about, she brings it up in any sports-related conversation to make people think that she has a clue. She doesn't.

I picked up on this one day when I heard her reference the team for the one hundredth time. I said to her, "You don't know shit about sports, do you?"

She said, "Of course, I do. Didn't you just hear what I said about the Mets?"

"That's the only team you ever talk about when people bring up sports."

Beat. Chelsea then walked away in her usual style—pretending to text. This is what she does when she's been caught at a lie and doesn't have the energy to maintain it. There is no way a person texts as much as Chelsea pretends to. It is just one more way for her to ignore and hide from the people she so often disappoints.

So when Chelsea realized that there was someone in the mix who didn't know that she was full of shit, she went in for the kill. She told my wife at a party that she'd won more than five hundred thousand dollars the year before gambling and that she bet on games every weekend.

"That's incredible," Beth said. "So, do you bet on everything?"

"Pretty much," Chelsea said. "I call my bookie once or twice a week. Last year I won so much that for tax purposes, I had to hide half a million dollars under my mattress. My business manager had me sit out last football season and I had to miss the play-offs. I'd never been more irate in my life."

I really believe that when Chelsea spins stories like this, she's almost waiting for you to call "bullshit." She pushes and pushes, expecting you at some point to tell her that she's full of crap and then she just moves on to the next target.

Back to that evening at Chelsea's house. After Beth believed her story about winning fifty thousand bucks, Chelsea got up and walked away, asking if anyone needed a drink. This was when my wife looked at me with her eyes as big as quarters and said, "Is that true?"

She turned to me to tell her the truth. She turned to me to lead her down the right path. She turned to me, and do you know what I said?

"Absolutely."

Fuck. Wait, what did I just say? Did I really just say "absolutely"? What was I thinking? I'll tell you what I was thinking, and it's an answer I think I gave a little earlier.

I'm an asshole.

Look, I love my wife—have her name tattooed on my finger—but I just couldn't help myself. It was instinct. And

I know some of you are thinking, *It's your instinct to lie?* No, that's not it at all, and that's what makes people like me different. The instinct isn't to lie; it's to fuck with people. Whenever we have Thanksgiving and all of my brothers are around, one of us always puts a plate in the oven for a long time, takes it out, and leaves it on the counter. Why? Because someone always picks it up, burns their hand, and drops it to the ground. It happens every year and it's funny every time. Is this male humor? Of course. Most women wouldn't find this entertaining in the least, but Chelsea would, and do you know why? Because Chelsea is a man. A man with really big tits.

Go for the joke and then let shit sort itself out afterward. Not always a great trait but, at the very least, it's entertaining.

By the end of the evening, I had almost forgotten about Chelsea's story. Since the joke had no real payoff, no big "Ha-ha! Joke's on you!" ending, I figured that it would just eventually fade away. I was wrong.

Two things I underestimated: Beth's sudden interest in gambling and Chelsea's love of fucking with people.

In the house I grew up in, for a prank to be worth it, there had to be a big payoff. Someone believing that you were a gambler when you weren't wouldn't have been enough. You would have had to make the other person bet and lose a shitload of cash or pretend to be in debt and hire fake mobsters to come over to the house to collect. Something where there were real consequences or you scared the living shit out of the other person.

But Chelsea is unique. The joy she gets out of even the little things puts her in a class all her own. Even if she has you believing something for only five seconds, it's fine with her. You can tell someone is truly into practical jokes if they don't need to be there when the payoff happens. Just the knowledge that it's going to happen is enough for Chelsea.

Then came our trip to the Bahamas. Chelsea chartered a ridiculous yacht for a group of people for three days. I couldn't have been more excited about the trip, and didn't consider for a second that Chelsea would use this as an opportunity to destroy my marriage. Every opportunity she had, she talked to Beth about gambling. How much she was winning, how easy it was for her, how she almost felt bad about "the gift" she had been given, blah, blah, blah. I had to walk away when I heard Chelsea say to Beth, "What's so crazy about all this is that I have so much good fortune already with the show and my books, and my tour, and then on top of that the universe rewards me with winning almost every bet I make on sports? Obviously someone upstairs is looking out for me." I couldn't fucking believe what I was hearing.

I had dug myself a bit of a hole.

If I had told my wife then, in the middle of paradise, at the apex of the nicest, most lavish weekend the two of us had ever been able to spend together, things would have gone downhill very quickly. The questions would have come at me fast and furious. "Why would you do that to me? What else do you lie to me about? How could you choose a joke over your wife?" All valid questions, none of which I had an answer to. I was screwed. You know who wasn't?

Chelsea.

It wasn't her responsibility to tell Beth the truth; it was mine. I've known Chelsea for ten years, and I've seen her pull her nonsense over and over. I've seen her persuade a drunk friend of mine whom she'd never met make a toast to a family member of mine he'd never met. I've seen her convince a driver in Cincinnati that she was in labor but absolutely needed to get some chicken nuggets from Wendy's before he dropped us off at the hotel, which— she also convinced him—had a pediatric unit. I've seen her convince a child that instead of being able to house children in her womb, she is able to house parakeets and certain reptiles.

It's usually hilarious to watch when it doesn't involve you or a loved one. Chelsea has this amazing way of enlisting you in her army. Partly because we love practical jokes and partly because you think that if you're in on it, you can't be the butt of it.

In the Bahamas, she was nonstop. Not just with Beth but with everyone. Her love of the five-second joke was evident all day every day. I can't remember the last time I laughed as hard as when she sprayed half a bottle of suntan lotion on someone's face and then had him stay still for pictures.

This is Geof Wills, who runs Chelsea's stand-up tours. He's the only person I know who's more immature than Chelsea.

This is Geof minus the lotion and minus the shirt. Chelsea brings him on vacations all the time just so she can photograph him with his shirt off and yell, "Watch out, fish!" every time he enters the water.

165

And remember the 1986 Mets? Well, one day we were going along the coast in a fishing boat when she started to tell everyone that all of the houses on that stretch of the beach were bought by the members of the 1986 Mets. She pointed to the houses and said things like "That's Darryl Strawberry's house, that's Doc Gooden's..." And people were all into it. They asked questions: "Why did they buy all of these houses down here?" "Did they really make that much money?"

"Of course they did," Chelsea said. "You don't win a World Series like that and not get hooked up with major endorsement money. Mookie Wilson has the biggest one. A lot of people don't know that he had the biggest contract." Her own agent, who is a huge sports fan, was sitting there staring at all the houses on the shoreline she was pointing at with his mouth gaping open like a Special Olympics champion.

Again, no huge payoff but enough to feed the beast. She delivered each line of bullshit like she was reading it out of the *1986 New York Mets Book of Facts*. She kept so many balls in the air that I couldn't imagine how she remembered all of them. She's very savant-like when she spews her nonsense. She rattles lies off so quickly and matter-of-factly that the people who have to gulp them up are usually so impressed by her knowledge they more often than not end up thanking her. That's the biggest joke of all.

There happened to be a horse race coming up, the Preakness, that my wife really wanted to bet on. She's

Chelsea kissing my wife in the Bahamas. I am in the background laughing at her baseball stats. You can see the evil look in Chelsea's eyes.

from Louisiana and there was a Cajun jockey who would be racing. Between the nostalgic feelings she had about her home state and Chelsea's "incredible" sports knowledge, Beth figured it was a sure thing. The entire weekend on the boat she and Chelsea talked about it and decided that when we got to New York they would place the bet.

I had to figure out a way not to lose this money. The two of them combined knew as much about horse racing as I do about tile flooring. (I'm a Jew.) As the horse race got closer, I did get a little lucky.

We were in New York for my performance at Radio City Music Hall. I think Chelsea performed that night, too, but I'm not 100 percent sure on that. The race was happening during the time we were all getting ready for the show and Chelsea was not (thank the Lord) answering her phone. Beth said she was going to place her bet anyway.

"Are you sure you wanna do that without talking to Chelsea?" I asked.

"Yup," she said. "I know how I want to bet and I'm just going to set up an online account."

"Huh?"

"I've been reading about it and there are lots of places I can just lay my bet online."

I was fucked. As I mentioned, my wife is a director, which means she researches shit. When she's into something, she wants to know everything there is to know on that subject. And her current subject was, unfortunately, betting. We had a bigger problem than I thought.

I had to figure a way out of this. *Wait, I know,* I thought. *How about I do something stupid like tell another lie?* Retard.

"Honey, why don't you go take a shower so you aren't rushed to get ready and I'll set up your account and place the bet."

"Uh...are you sure?"

She was nervous for two reasons. One, I am a technological idiot. Don't know how to do anything with computers at all. Besides porn and ESPN.com, the Interweb is like a foreign language to me. The second reason she was nervous was that I always break electronics. I don't have a metal plate in my head or anything, but there is something in my body that fucks shit up. My cell phone crashes all the time, remotes break, brand-new DVD players stop working, and, most of all, laptops shit the bed. This time, I would just claim that it had happened again and there was no way to set up the account.

"I can do it," I said. "Just take your shower."

"Okay, but hurry. There's only fifteen minutes until the race starts."

Perfect.

So while she was in the shower I sat there, watched TV, and right when I heard the water stop, yelled, "What is going on?" and took the battery out of the computer.

Beth came out of the bathroom in a towel. "What's wrong?"

I told her that the computer had just stopped working. She came over, tried to turn it on, and said, "I knew I should have done it myself."

And with that, she went into the other room to get ready for the show and watch the race. She didn't yell and she didn't make any snide comments, but I knew she was angry. That's how nice she is. I figured she'd be angry right up until the race ended, and when her horse lost she would thank me for being too stupid to work a computer and realize that gambling just wasn't for her.

And then the race started.

And then her horse won.

Big time.

And then she came storming out of the room.

And then my phone rang.

It was Chelsea. "Can I talk to Beth?"

"No."

"Is that Chelsea?" Beth said. "Let me talk to her. Give me the phone! Hello? I know. I can't believe it! No, I didn't because Josh broke the computer... We did call but nobody answered... How much? You won $200,000?" Beth's face dropped, but she managed to muster a "That's unbelievable! I can't believe I missed out on it either!" she said, glaring at me again. "Okay, see you tonight."

I apologized profusely to my wife, but she just stared into space for a few minutes. "I would've won five thousand dollars, Josh. Dammit."

Not only did I feel awful, but I was starting to feel a little *Black Swan*-y. My mind was racing back and forth trying to distinguish fact from fiction. I couldn't grasp if my wife would truly have won the money or if Chelsea was rigging sporting events all across the globe. I kept reminding myself of what was real and what wasn't, but eventually I had to sit down. When we were both able to pull ourselves together, we met Chelsea at a Belvedere event she had to go to that night.

She and Beth made plans to bet on an upcoming horse race, and I had no credibility to stop it because if I had actually set up the account, Beth would have won. The thing is, I knew I had to stop her, because I am a gambler. I lose money every weekend during football season, and the one thing I know is, no matter how "prepared"

170

you think you are, no matter how much you research the games, you're gonna lose. Problem with that? The more knowledgeable you are about the sport, the more you chase your money. Don't believe me? Ask my bookie or the Las Vegas casinos that seem to spring up quicker than herpes at a *Chelsea Lately* staff off site.

The only way to stop it was to tell Beth the truth, which was gonna suck nuts for me. I was completely at fault. I hadn't stopped the joke because I'd figured it would stop itself, but, no, it had just kept spiraling and spiraling. She was gonna be pissed, and rightly so. I had allowed her to be led astray for weeks and had never said anything. I had betrayed her trust. But what was I supposed to do? Wait until she lost money and then tell her about the joke? There was gonna be a fight. A big one. The worst kind of fight, mind you; the kind I couldn't win.

I decided to wait until the end of the week and then take her on a nice weekend to Santa Barbara. I figured that sometime on the drive up there, she would forgive me because I'm a dumbass and the weekend together would just put a bow on it. I told Chelsea that I was going to tell Beth about the joke and maybe to expect a tiny little shit storm, but nothing too bad.

When Friday came, I told Beth I needed to talk to her, but she said she really needed to tell me something first. Knowing that I was delivering nothing she wanted to hear, I decided I should probably build up as much goodwill as I could, so I let her do the honors.

"I lost ten thousand dollars," she said.

Uh...what? I'm sorry, it sounded like you said you lost ten thousand dollars, but I know there's no way that's possible, because we don't have ten thousand dollars for you to lose. I know some of you are thinking, "What do you mean you don't have ten thousand dollars to lose? That's nothing. You're on TV and rich." One of those is true. Let's just say that with a lot of my checks, after I pay The Man, my agent, lawyer, and manager, I barely have enough left over to get drunk. But make no mistake: ten thousand dollars is a lot of fucking money.

"I don't understand," I said. "How did you lose ten thousand dollars?"

"Well, Chelsea and I bet on a basketball game last week and won." What? They bet a basketball game last week? How did I not know about that? "We bet one more Monday and won." What in the fuck is going on here? "So, I thought I would try one on my own, and I lost. I'm so sorry, baby. I don't know what I was thinking. I was winning. It all seemed so easy, like I could never lose."

Oh. My. God. This was not the conversation I thought *I* was going to have. Ten thousand dollars?

I called Chelsea. "Beth lost ten thousand dollars."

Silence.

"Did you hear what I said?"

"I heard you," she responded. "That's not good."

"No shit that's not good. Why were you guys gambling?"

"Well, every fake bet I made I would have won, so I thought I'd try a couple of real ones," she explained. "Beth kept calling and calling about when we were betting, so I let her bet with me. Ten thousand dollars. Wow. That's a lot of money. I'll call you back."

Fifteen minutes later I got this text: It's not $10K. It's $15K. His name is Trent. 310-xxx-xxxx. I'm really sorry about this."

Great. Fifteen thousand I didn't have that I needed to shell over to a bookie. So I called him. I figured I could explain the situation and tell him that I'd pay it off in two installments. Now, I've been around enough bookies to know that normally there's no way they would let that happen, but I figured I would drop Chelsea's name and the guy would cut me some slack. I'll cut right to the only quote you need to know from that conversation.

"I don't care if you're friends with the Pope. It's fifteen K all at the same time."

There was no getting out of this. Fifteen thousand dollars basically would wipe out my little cushion. But as much as we couldn't afford to pay this guy, we had to pay this guy. Trent didn't strike me as a dude who was going to let $15K just walk away. The next day, I set up a time to go over to his house and then went to the bank to get the money.

You ever write a check big enough for you not to want to let go of it? Imagine that . . . but with cash. I had fifteen thousand dollars in cash in my hand. I'd be lying if I told you the idea of driving to Mexico and seeing how long I could be drunk off $15K didn't at least flash through my mind. And by flash, I mean I thought about it for about twenty-five minutes.

I drove up to Trent's house in the Hollywood Hills; he buzzed me in at the gate and told me that he was in the back by the pool. As I was walking around the house all I could think was how I'd dug my own grave on this one. I never spoke up and because of that I was out $15K. I also decided that, to save my own ass, I would never tell Beth about the joke. *Ever.* That was the one good thing. She felt she had to make it up to me because she was the one who'd fucked up.

Nothing in the world could've prepared me for what I saw when I turned the corner and entered Trent's backyard. It was Chelsea and Beth. Sitting on chairs by the pool.

"What's up, asshole?" Chelsea said.

I was too stunned to speak.

They had set me up from the beginning. As soon as I had told Beth that Chelsea was a big-time gambler, Chelsea pulled the ol' switcheroo. That tricky bitch.

Who knows? Maybe I am adopted.

Josh should be ashamed of himself. His wife is the sweetest person I have ever met, and it's unfortunate he found himself in such a jam. I believe I am singlehandedly responsible for saving their marriage. Godspeed.

—Chelsea

This is Josh with my sisters. Everyone has a crush on Josh except for me—because we almost went down that road ten years ago until both of us made sharp turns in opposite directions.

Chapter Eight

Sisterly Love

SHOSHANNA HANDLER

My name is Shoshanna and I am Chelsea's older sister. My parents told me that before Chelsea was born I was a cute, good-natured, happy-go-lucky kid. Then came 1975 and my blissful little five-year-old world was turned

Chelsea and me on our front lawn in New Jersey. This was before our relationship went south.

176

upside down. I had been the baby of our large and dysfunctional family for five years and had loved every minute of it. I didn't know what to make of the new addition to our family, or why they would have named her Chelsea. Every time I heard her name, it reminded me of seafood stew. I cried all the time.

Chelsea had an all-consuming presence. It felt like being hit by a train. My father has told us all many times over that when she was born, she came out with such a strong cry that the nurse said to him, "You'd better watch out for this one." Over the years, I became more quiet and pensive as Chelsea's boisterous personality took center stage. She was full of piss and vinegar from day one, and could throw a tantrum that would put any toddler to shame. This kid was a force to be reckoned with, and my parents were already exhausted with their other five kids. They were in no way prepared to handle raising this particular child, and their feeble efforts were of little consequence. Besides, our mom was always napping, knitting, or cooking, and was too soft-spoken to really stand up to Chelsea.

By the time Chelsea was three, she had the street smarts of a nine-year-old, and I may as well have been born yesterday. We were complete opposites, like oil and water, and never agreed on anything. If I was watching a TV show she didn't like, she would say something like "A package just came for you at the door, Shana," or "Mom just took some brownies out of the oven," and then take over the television. I fell for it every time. I would come back in the room and wage war in the form of a wrestling match. Ultimately I would be the one to get yelled at or sent to my room because I was "older" and "should know better." We fought constantly and wanted to rip each other's throats out for most of our childhood. Physically I had the upper hand, but verbally I was no match for her. By the time she was eight, she had the debating skills of a seasoned politician, and I am being completely serious.

For many years we shared a bedroom, and we agreed to place masking tape down the middle and not cross territories. This was pretty much a joke, unless we were both in the room. Raids occurred when the other person was not there. Chelsea would regularly steal my clothes when I was in high school. (Yes, it's true, she's five years younger, and we were clearly different sizes, but this did not deter her. She would just knot the shirts at the waist or cut them in half.) At one point I installed latches to hold a combination lock on my closet door. A week later I came home from school to find her wearing the brand-new clothes I had just purchased with my first paycheck from my new afterschool job at the mall. I went nuts and ran upstairs to find that she had taken a screwdriver to the latches. And because she was so angry I wouldn't share with her, she decided to tie-dye all my underwear.

Years later, when Chelsea was about fifteen and I was twenty and home from college, it was with great joy that I picked up the phone and heard a police officer tell me that they had Chelsea down at the station for shoplifting underwear at Sears with a friend. Underwear has always been a big theme in our family. Not wearing any can and *has* resulted in humiliation, in the form of photographs, e-mails, and/or having you and your genitalia chased around the house with salad tongs.

My parents weren't home the day I got the call, and if I went and picked Chelsea up and kept it under wraps, she would owe me big time. I drove very slowly down to the police station with a big old grin on my face. I had had a good time at college, but this would definitely be the highlight of my life since graduating from high school. I was still smiling when I got to the police station and Chelsea got in the car.

It didn't take her long to pronounce, "I know what you're thinking, and I'd rather tell Mom and Dad the truth than be beholden to you for anything. So if you think you're going to pull something over on me, you're mistaken. I would rather lose my virginity to Craig Slass than owe you a favor." Craig Slass was our next-door neighbor, who would easily have had sex with any one of us, if we had permitted it. He spat when he talked, was always drooling, and had what Chelsea referred to as a "woman's ass."

Our parents had a modest second home on Martha's Vineyard, and every summer, as soon as school let out, our mom would head up there with all of us six kids and whatever dog we had at the time, in our awful van with blue vinyl bench seats. We would spend the entire summer there each year. Our father would come up every ten days or so and stay four or five days and then return to his bustling used-car business in New Jersey.

One summer on the Vineyard, I told Chelsea we were setting up a lemonade stand at the end of our dirt road so we could make a little extra spending money. I was twelve and she was seven. Things at the stand were hopping for an hour or so, and then sales fell flat. Chelsea, clearly bored, thought we should spice things up with a big sign for a raffle to meet Carly Simon, who lived on the Vineyard, too, but whom we did not know.

"It will get things moving around here," she said.

"But that would be a lie, Chels..."

"So what? No one is going to actually win the raffle, retard."

"But what if the police come around? I don't know about this." I was always a big worrier.

She looked at me with disgust. "The Martha's Vineyard Police are not concerned with the two of us, Shoshanna. They have bigger problems than a twelve- and a seven-year-old selling lemonade and fake raffle tickets. Why are you such a Debbie Downer?" This was what Chelsea called me, and still calls me to this day when I bring up a point she doesn't think is necessary to discuss.

Things did pick up a little with the raffle sign prominently displayed. We found ourselves fielding a lot of questions about Carly Simon, but Chelsea was always fast on her feet and had an answer for everything. I let her handle it. Of course, some of her answers were ridiculous, but who was going to challenge a seven-year-old?

At one point, a lady on a bike stopped and bought a

Chelsea and me at our lemonade stand.

lemonade and a raffle ticket and asked us if we thought Carly might sing for her if she won the raffle. Chelsea replied, "Not too many people know this, but Carly has very bad stage fright. You have to catch her on the right day. Some days she'll sing and some days she won't. It depends which way the wind blows."

Another woman asked when she would be able to meet Carly Simon, since she was on Martha's Vineyard for only a few weeks. "It's not a problem," Chelsea assured her. "Carly and I are very tight. She's on tour right now, but I am in constant contact with her manager, and I am sure we can set something up." The look on this woman's face was priceless.

After another hour went by, things were dead again.

181

It was then that Chelsea "accidentally" knocked over the change jar, pocketed most of the money when I wasn't looking, and said she had to go to the bathroom and would be right back. She did not return. I ended up having to cart the table, chairs, signs, and pitchers on our red wagon solo down the very long dirt road back to the house. I later found out that Chelsea had hightailed it with our money into town on her banana-seat bike and treated herself to a buttered bagel and a Coke and then blew the rest of the dough at the arcade. You might think that no parent would have allowed their seven-year-old to ride into town alone on a bike and hang out. Well, with my parents it was pretty much a free-for-all, and it was 1982 and things were pretty loosey-goosey on the Vineyard. We hitchhiked all the time and it was no big deal. We never would have dreamed of doing this back in New Jersey, but for some reason, on the Vineyard, it was okay.

When she got back, I yelled at Chelsea and told my parents what she had done. Chelsea said lemonade stands were for chumps and the real money was in babysitting.

"Hello, who is going to let us babysit? We are way too young," I replied.

"Listen, Shana, if you lost your goody-two-shoes looks, we could easily get you up to age fourteen. I could pass for ten. I'll say I'm your assistant, and we'll split the profits sixty/forty. Sixty for me, since it's my idea." Chelsea had already inherited some of my used-car-dealer father's warped reasoning, and it was maddening to deal with.

"Maybe in a few years, girls, not just yet," my mother wisely chimed in. "Stick with the lemonade stand for now."

We had three older teenage brothers, and when we were up on the Vineyard, they got to sleep in the basement. The basement was the cool place to be. It had a separate entrance, its own bathroom, and a little fridge. It was like a clubhouse. My brothers' names were painted on the walls, and there was thick shaggy carpeting and bunk beds everywhere. My brothers had a stereo and a million records and were usually playing Cat Stevens, Neil Young, or the Grateful Dead. There were even a couple of bongs down there, but we didn't know what they were at the time. At least, *I* didn't. Mom told us they were microscopes. She was completely clueless about drugs.

Our brothers had jobs during the summer, so they were often gone during the day. Chelsea and I would go down there and snoop around when we got bored. One day I found a rubber snake in my brothers' stuff. Chelsea was and always has been petrified of snakes. She could not even see one on TV without crying hysterically. At the time, I'd had a rough few days of Chelsea's shenanigans, and I wanted revenge. For weeks she had been daring me to drive an old two-door Datsun around our dirt road while my mother took her daily nap. It was a beater car that my dad left on the island year round. Chelsea had kept egging me on, calling me Goody Two-shoes and saying I was a giant sissy and that she would get her driver's license before I did. I was sick of her teasing and finally drove the car just to shut her up, but of course, I dented the door on a big tree branch in the process. My father came up to the island the next day and went off on me, as Chelsea smiled devilishly behind him.

Before bedtime that night I took the rubber snake I had found earlier in my brothers' room and put it under Chelsea's pillow. She climbed into bed, snuggled in, felt the snake, then saw it and went apeshit. Bloodcurdling screams could be heard up to a mile away. She was absolutely hysterical and practically having a seizure while hyperventilating at the same time. I had a hollow feeling in the pit of my stomach. This wasn't good. I hadn't really thought this one through.

I was screaming, "It's just a toy, it's fake, it's fake, okay?!" I could hear footsteps approaching quickly and they sounded ominous. I tried to cover Chelsea's mouth so no one would hear her. She kicked me in the coslopus, wrestled me off her, and literally slid down the stairs and into the main living room, with her ass bouncing off each step. My mother was already rounding the corner when I got to the bottom step. I looked up just in time to see my mom's hand reach out and slap me across the face. She didn't even ask what had happened; she could tell from Chelsea's reaction that it had to have been something bad.

Chelsea was yelling, "Sn...sn...sna...ke!!" She sounded like the girl in *Jaws* yelling, "Shark," but worse. It was the only time my mother had ever hit me. Until that day, my parents smacked Chelsea all the time, but they had never hit me. I think they felt sorry for me, and I appreciated their pity.

For many weeks following the snake incident I had rocks, dirt, or sand under my own pillow to welcome me each night.

Once Chelsea was a full-fledged teenager, our relationship hit new lows. She thought I was a band geek pansy and about as exciting as a sixty-year-old librarian. I thought she was a possessed and troubled degenerate on the fast track to trouble. We had absolutely nothing in common. I was very easily embarrassed, so she would yell "Bertha" at me in public and make everyone stop and look at us. It was horrifying, and basically the only time she spoke to me aside from swearing at me. She thought it was hysterical, and loved to see me squirm. We just couldn't stand each other, and we even went through a couple of years when we didn't speak to each other at all. She also raised hell with my parents.

The completion of her bat mitzvah was a miracle in itself. My brothers all had wagers with one another on whether it was actually going to take place. Most kids prepare for a couple of years. Chelsea regularly skipped her sessions with the cantor and rabbi. They had never in all their years at the temple worked with a child like her before. She regularly swore at them, she was always defiant, never prepared, and repeatedly said she wasn't going to practice until a week before the ceremony. At one point, she slammed down the Torah and exclaimed that all this was practically child abuse, because she wasn't ready to commit to having a bat mitzvah and wasn't even sure she wanted to be a Jew. It wasn't pretty, but in the end she somehow managed to pull it off without making any mistakes. This, of course, drove me insane, as I was silently hoping she would embarrass herself the way she had embarrassed me so many times, but on a bigger scale. Pure schadenfreude. Google it.

It wasn't until I was twenty-four that I became determined to repair my relationship with Chelsea. I was single, living on my own in Seattle, and working as a registered nurse. I really wanted to take a trip to Hawaii, and I wanted Chelsea to come with me. Admittedly, I was a bit of a late bloomer, but I was finally ready to sow my wild oats. I thought maybe this trip would be a fresh start for Chelsea and me. We would rebuild our sisterly foundation on a big adventure—just the two of us.

I very excitedly called her up. "Chelsea!" I said, bursting at the seams. "Let's go to Hawaii for a few days. I will pay for everything. It'll be a blast, and I am sure you could use a few days off." At the time, Chelsea was living in LA with our aunt and uncle, nine cousins, and six animals in a three-bedroom bungalow. She was waiting tables and auditioning in Hollywood.

My proposition was met with a long silence on the other end of the line. "Can I think about it and call you back?" she asked.

"Chelsea, really? You won't go with me on vacation to Hawaii?"

"Shana, no offense, but you are not my idea of a good time."

"I know, but I'm more fun now, and I promise we won't fight. I'll even promise to drink with you." I had never been a big drinker, and Chelsea considered nondrinkers very untrustworthy.

Finally, she said, "Well, as much as going on a trip with you seems like watching paint dry, I could really use a break. Hawaii sounds pretty good actually. But you'd better cool it, Shana. Your enthusiasm is a little alarming. We are not planning a honeymoon here or going on a bunch of gay tours. I just want to chill out and relax. And drink."

"Okay, okay," I said. Chelsea probably had no intention of doing anything other than getting a borderline amazing tan and hooking up with a semi-hot Samoan dude, but I would try to wear her down. "Chelsea, we can't go all the way to Hawaii and not even go to a luau. It would be sacrilegious." I reminded her: "The drinks will be free-flowing, it's only a couple of hours, and don't forget, I'm picking up the tab for the whole trip."

About six weeks later we took a red-eye flight to Hawaii. On the way, I made friends with my seatmate; she and I talked the whole way there. I knew Chelsea was farting, and I told her to knock it off. Near the end of the flight I got my new friend's phone number, but when I went to the bathroom, Chelsea ripped it up.

"What the hell did you do that for?" I said.

"Well," Chelsea said, "two reasons, really. Number one, you didn't shut the fuck up the entire flight. It's a red-eye, but thanks to you I didn't get any sleep. And number two is for accusing me of farting on a flight. Shame on you, Debbie. Shame on you."

We stepped out of the airport and hailed a taxi. In Oahu, or any tropical destination for that matter, any hotel worth squat is on the beach. I know that now. Back then, however, I thought *near* the beach was good enough, right? Plus I would save a few bucks. As our taxi started heading away from the beach, Chelsea yelled, "What is happening? We are in Hawaii, I just spent what seemed like four years on a plane, and now the beach is disappearing. Shana! What is going on? Where the hell are we staying?" she screamed.

"Oh... well, I got a great deal at this place in town. It's just a half mile walk to the beach."

"Oh, that sounds fabulous," she mumbled.

We pulled up to the Grand Hotel (not so grand) and I hit the driver with my big tip (not). Later Chelsea lit into me about the standards and practices of tipping. Since she'd joined the service industry as a waitress in LA, tipping had become a very sensitive issue for her. My low tip evidently was unacceptable and not to be repeated. To this day, you are not to argue with Chelsea when she hands you a ridiculous amount of money to give to a waitress, hotel employee, or concierge at a hotel. I'm not rich, and I'd be lying if I said I haven't thought about pocketing some of the money she's instructed me to hand out to people on islands we will never see again.

After getting a few hours of sleep, I suggested we check out the hotel pool. We headed up to the cement rooftop pool and made a quick U-turn. It was not a pretty picture: a bunch of beer-bellied, bald, leering assholes in the Jacuzzi and a pool of questionable water color. Upon seeing all this, Chelsea decided to take the reins on our daily plans. She told me we were hoofing it to Waikiki Beach and to put on my walking shoes. I wasn't much for exercise or exerting any kind of physical energy, but I agreed, only after she told me my bathing suit looked a little too snug in the rear. Her exact words were "Your ass looks like Delta Burke trying to crawl through a tennis racket."

After much complaining on my part and both of us sweating like pigs carrying our crap to the beach in ninety-plus-degree heat, we finally arrived. Chelsea scoped out a decent-looking hotel on the beach with a great pool and a guest population that appeared to be under forty. "Shana, let's find our spot. Don't worry, we'll blend right in," she assured me.

"I really don't know about this, Chelsea," I said.

I grabbed two chaise lounges close to the pool, and we set up shop and caught some rays. We got pretty hungry and figured we should try to order some food. I picked out a few items on the menu, and Chelsea signaled the waiter to give him our order.

He asked for our room number and she blurted out, "Twelve twenty-one." I, a rotten liar, felt uncomfortable. The waiter looked at the two of us suspiciously but finally walked away.

"Shana, what's the matter with you? Just go with the flow."

Our food arrived, and a short time later the waiter came back and said that there must be some mistake with our room number. "I am going to have to see your room key, miss."

"Oh, I am so sorry, there must be a misunderstanding. Maybe I got the number backward or something." Chelsea rifled through her bag, as though she were looking for the key. I was shaking in my flip-flops and not being much of a wing woman. Chelsea was going to have to handle this solo. "You know what? I can't believe it, but I think I lost it swimming at the beach earlier. How about if we just pay in cash?"

"This pool and bar are for hotel guests only, miss," the waiter said.

"Are you accusing us of crashing this pool?" Chelsea said. "I mean, really, I find that very offensive. I am going to have to talk to the manager about the awful treatment we are receiving here." She probably could have pulled this off, but I had blown our cover. Tears started to well up in my eyes, and Chelsea looked at me with horror.

"Are you seriously crying?"

"I'll be right back," the waiter said and left.

"Okay, Shana, let's hit it. Grab your shit and nonchalantly walk to the beach," Chelsea whispered. Over my shoulder I could see our waiter with two large security guards on either side of him heading toward our spot. They were both ridiculously overweight, so I wasn't worried about outrunning them, but I wasn't fast enough for Chelsea. "Step it up! They are onto us!" They started running after us, but we were able to lose them fairly quickly.

190

That was too much excitement for me already, but when you're with Chelsea, there's always more to come. We found a nice spot on the beach, and Chelsea said we were both looking pretty pale and should forgo the sunscreen to get a jump on our tans. She also forced me to join her in having a piña colada, which resulted in our quickly falling asleep for a few hours. We spent the next two days holed up in our crappy hotel room treating extremely severe cases of sunburn. We were in agony and were ridiculously red. Chelsea rationed off a few Percocet she had been saving for a rainy day and we watched a marathon of Lifetime movies until we reemerged.

Day four was, much to my sister's dismay, luau time. Chelsea was bitching about it all day, but I had already paid for it and wasn't about to let her forget that. Besides, I had a feeling I was going to meet Prince Charming there.

When we boarded the bus, though, it appeared as if we had just been admitted to a nursing home.

"Are you fucking kidding me?" Chelsea said, loud enough for everyone to hear. "What kind of luau is this? There isn't a single person on this bus under seventy. Shana, you signed us up for a senior citizens' luau? You are such a moron. I will never go anywhere with you ever again, do you understand me? And good fucking luck finding your soul mate."

After she calmed down a bit, she decided to have a little fun and make me pay. She put her arm around my shoulder and struck up a conversation with the ladies across the

aisle. "Hi y'all! I'm Fannie and this here is Bertha, my lesbian lover. We are just so doggone happy to be going on
this trip. Are you two ladies together, too? This is the lesbian luau, right?"

I knew I was turning different shades of fuchsia because
my red was all used up.

All night long, Chelsea told anyone who would listen
stories about how we'd met and what our hobbies were.
The stories were absolutely ludicrous, and every time she
said "Bertha," I stiffened up. She told one couple that we'd
met at the Junior Olympics when we were both on the
young women's high dive team. She interspersed all of
this banter with a quick kiss on my lips, and whenever I
refused, she pinched me severely under the table. I am sure
it was pretty rewarding for her to see me so unnerved.

I didn't think she could keep up this charade, but as the
night wore on she was clearly getting into it; I noticed her
lesbian accent was improving greatly. She had gathered quite
a crowd around her for her description of our "African safari"
trip the year before to visit a special lesbian animal reserve.
The highlight of that fake trip was her saving my life. I was
supposedly picked up in the trunk of a lesbian elephant. The
elephant wouldn't put me down, and started to trot off with
me, while I screamed and cried. Everyone in the luau group
was staring at me incredulously. Then Chelsea topped it off
with "I just had to save her any way I could. Bertha was my
soul mate, and so I ran after that elephant and launched a
gourd at its ass, and that was that. Bertha tumbled to the

ground like a house of cards." The tale was just preposterous, and as per usual, I was at a total loss for words. Chelsea was so good at telling the story that these people actually believed her. Many came up to me afterward and expressed how lucky I was to have Fannie in my life.

On the bus ride home she said, "Payback's a bitch, isn't it, Bertha?"

But I wasn't ready to give up on my vacation yet. I still wanted to hit Hanauma Bay, a supposed prime snorkeling spot. When we got there I noticed that almost everyone on the beach was Japanese and armed with a snorkel and a camera. People were staring at us and taking photos, and then they started coming toward us one by one, asking

Chelsea at the luau. She was twenty-one in this photo but looks forty-five. She does really look like a lesbian in those pants.

if Chelsea would be in a picture with them. This was long before Chelsea was on TV or had written a book, so naturally I was confused by the attention they were giving her.

"What the fuck?" Chelsea said.

"Don't you see, Chelsea? They think you're Pamela Anderson. You're blonde and you're wearing a red bathing suit. They love *Baywatch* in Japan."

The situation was completely ridiculous, and Chelsea really got a kick out of it. She decided to go with the flow, as people started shoving me out of the way to get close to her. Chelsea was really getting into it, posing for photos and actually signing Pam Anderson autographs for people. Most of them just spoke Japanese, but one lady said she worked for a newspaper and wanted to know if "Pam" would answer a few questions.

"Sure, why not?" Chelsea said with a smile.

"What are you doing here in Oahu, Pam?" the lady asked.

"Well, actually I am here doing some research for *Baywatch*. We were thinking about doing a Christmas special in Hawaii on a great beach like this. I am here with my assistant to see if this really will fit with our idea for the show. Unfortunately, we have to get back in a couple of days to finish this season's finale. No more questions, please, I feel a bit tired. Thank you, thank you."

"You really are unbelievable, you know that?" I said. "You might get sued for doing what you just did."

"Oh please, get a grip, Shana!" Chelsea said, laughing. "It was funny, and good practice actually, as I plan to become a great actress one day, so you'd better get used to it."

The only thing left to make the trip complete was the flight back home, during which I got airsick and unloaded my lunch in my airsickness bag, on my shorts, and on Chelsea's new skirt.

The bonding vacation didn't turn out exactly as I had planned, and I was pretty sure Chelsea would not consider traveling with me again anytime soon. I consoled myself with a memory from when I was in the sixth grade and she was in the first. The neighborhood bully decided to target me one day for the factory-reject corduroys my parents had sprung for. Chelsea marched over to this big kid without any hesitation, got right in his face as best she could, being only six and a half years old, and said, "Listen up, fat ass. I have two things to tell you. One, you'd better leave my sister alone or I'm gonna break your dog's neck, and two, I hope you choke on a Twinkie."

Whether she felt disdain for me or not, Chelsea always had my back, and a pretty big set of balls—which is true to this day. She still reminds me of what a buzz kill I am, and still has me listed in her phone as "Debbie Downer," but once Chelsea started making money, she became much easier for me to get along with. After that luau, she has never stopped kissing me hard on the lips, and always in inappropriate situations. The only thing that's changed is that I've stopped fighting it.

My sister Shana still has room for improvement. She is constantly tired and constantly asking extremely annoying questions. I like her more now than I did when we were younger, and I definitely love her more now than I did when I was younger. We talk all the time and vacation together all the time, but I'd be lying if I said we'd be friends if she weren't my sister. We would not.

—Chelsea

Shana giving it to me from behind in Atlantic City.

Chapter Nine

Eva Is My Name, Comedy Is My Game

EVA MAGDALENSKI

The first time I met Chelsea I was nineteen. I was working at the Denver Comedy Club and she was there performing for the week. I immediately loved her. I didn't necessarily think that she was that funny, but she seemed smart and quick. I also really loved the fluorescent scrunchies she wore in her hair. Sometimes a well-dressed ponytail is all it takes to get me going, and don't even get me started on how I feel about an organized French braid. Since then, Chelsea has ditched the scrunchies, but there are some memories that nobody can take away from me.

While Chelsea was in Denver, she had to go to several radio stations and give on-air interviews to promote her shows. It was my responsibility to make sure she made it to those stations and that she was comfortable.

You know that feeling you get when someone comes up to you and starts massaging your shoulders without asking first? You become very still and uncertain while the unwelcome massage quickly becomes kind of creepy and uncomfortable. All you can think about is how badly you want that person's hands off you. You can't really function or make any sudden movements without making things really awkward, so all you say is "Oh, thanks...you don't have to do that. No, really. That's okay. Please. Get off me."

Well, I was giving Chelsea those massages during her radio interviews. My intention was to relax her; it was early in the morning and from what I'd seen with other stand-up comics over the years, there was a good chance she was hungover. Luckily, instead of getting irritated and shouting, "Stranger danger!" the way many had in the past, Chelsea appeared to enjoy my famous touch. She said it was really weird that I had no boundaries when it came to molesting her shoulders, and she appreciated someone who didn't care if they made other people uncomfortable. After that she lovingly nicknamed me Sloppy Sea Bass. I don't know what that had to do with the massage, but coming from Chelsea, that nickname was a sign of affection.

Chelsea liked something else about me, but when I recently asked her to tell me what that "something" was, she said she'd have to get back to me. One thing that Chelsea did recognize about me was that I had a passion for comedy. I guess I didn't hide it all that well, since all I talked about was my passion for comedy. I've often been told that I don't have much of a life, but the joke is on the people who say that to me, because the fact is I don't. But at least I'm aware of it.

She also enjoyed my sense of humor. One day I went to use the restroom and noticed that Chelsea was in the stall next to mine. When I heard another person enter the bathroom, I started yelling, "What is all of this blood? There's so much blood!" Chelsea exited her stall and the bathroom, completely ignoring me and leaving the stranger to deal with my pretend situation. Ten minutes later, Chelsea offered me a job as her publicist.

Working at a comedy club in Denver was enjoyable, but there wasn't a ton of room to move up the ladder. At best I would have become head waitress one day. I was pretty eager to get my career going, so I accepted Chelsea's offer and quit the club. I began working as her eager—probably overeager—publicist. It was hard work, but it was fun. I was still living in Denver, and she was in Los Angeles, which was fine, since most of the work I needed to do could be done from a phone or computer. We got along really well, which Chelsea says may have had something to do with the long-distance thing. In any case, we developed a pretty close relationship; it was like a sisterhood minus the traveling pants.

Then Chelsea got an offer to host her own show. Since she recognized over the years that I was a hard worker who also happened to have amazing breath, she offered me a full-time job as her assistant. I accepted and moved to Los Angeles. She generously allowed me to move in with her and her boyfriend while I got settled in the city and looked for my own place. She told me to keep an eye out for a place for her as well, because she hated her boyfriend. After a couple of months of living with them, Chelsea told me to get out while I could. She saw no reason that we both needed to suffer through her current living situation.

"I'll be free soon," she told me. "See you on the other side."

I took her advice and settled into my new apartment in a new city and started concentrating on my new job. It was unbelievable: my most likely dead-end job at a comedy club had turned into my dream job with a comedian who was on the verge of huge things. It took only a couple of weeks of working that closely with her for it to become clear to me that Chelsea Handler was, and still is, a huge con artist.

Before I moved to Los Angeles I knew nothing about fashion, television, or celebrity. Now I know a lot about celebrity, but I still wear stretch pants and ill-fitting shirts. However, stand-up comedy was and is still my main area of expertise. That's where the whole "having no life" thing comes from. When you stay in on weekend nights watching old Steve Martin videos, it's hard to convince others that you have a ton going on. Any opportunity I had to show off the skills I did have, I took. I was probably a little overzealous with my knowledge. A simple mention of the word *comedy* by someone, and I would butt in: "Stand-up? What do you want to know about stand-up? I pretty much know everything about every comic ever. Heard of the Denver Comedy Club? I ran it, kind of!"

My reputation as resident comedy expert was really flourishing around the offices of *Chelsea Lately*. I walked around with my head held high. That was also because Chelsea told me I had horrible posture and had more than once threatened to make me wear a back brace. I felt I had even garnered a lot of respect from the camera crew; from what I could tell, they didn't respect much, so I felt pretty special—until someone stole the plaque that hung on my office door. I had proudly made it myself, very carefully embossing in gold the words "Eva: Comedy Expert," and I buffed it daily with a gentle cloth. I was bummed when it was taken, but I refused to make a big deal out of it. Besides, I had a backup over my gas fireplace at home.

There was only one person who didn't take me seriously. He was Chelsea's personal appearance agent, and he was never interested in what I had to say. He, whom we shall call Rick because it rhymes with what I used to whisper under my breath every time I saw him, always blatantly disregarded my very valuable insights and understanding of how to market Chelsea's stand-up career. He never responded to my text messages or e-mails, or confirmed that he had received any of my numerous smoke signals. He never even bothered to call me back to discuss my brilliant idea of selling scratch-'n'-sniff panties with Chelsea's face on them or life jackets that read "Chelseahandler.com" for her summer appearances. I felt the latter was both useful and promotional, not to mention life-saving. It's also never been done before. In fact, I'm glad I reminded myself about them, because they still need to be made. Eva: 1, Rick: 0.

No matter what people might think about me, and I've heard some pretty awful things, when it comes to Chelsea, I know what I'm talking about. I've done more than my fair share to keep myself informed on everything about her. I have spent many a night putting articles, photos, and ticket stubs into scrapbooks. I prefer to complete them monthly, so that at the end of the year she will have twelve lovely books of memories to flip through and help her reflect on what she has accomplished over the months. I like to think she sits down with them on New Year's Day over a bowl of black-eyed peas, perhaps while listening to the Black Eyed Peas, and congratulates herself on a job well done while compiling a list of all the things she would like to accomplish in the coming year. Unfortunately, Chelsea walked into my office one day during an all-out scrapbooking session. Seeing me sitting on the floor and sweating while surrounded by photos of her, with scissors in one hand and glitter in the other, and wearing a ChelseaHandler.com life vest must have been too much for her to handle.

She said to me, "Eva, this is where I draw the line. I've seen *Single White Female*, and I'm not interested in you putting a stiletto through one of my lover's eyes. No more fucking scrapbooks."

"But, Chelsea, this year has been so—"

"Eva, stop. This is what people do when they are children.

I never did it because, for the most part, my childhood is something I'd like to forget. If you put together one more of those things, I'm going to cut your hair off at the ponytail."

Chelsea knew how much I loved a good ponytail, and the idea of no longer being able to wear a side one sent me into the fetal position. I put away my glue stick and double-sided tape and decided to focus on getting Rick to make a nice new poster for Chelsea's upcoming shows.

I tried to do everything I could to help Rick help Chelsea succeed, but he ignored me. He consistently sent out old

You'll notice that Chelsea is about ten pounds overweight in this photo.

promotional materials for Chelsea's stand-up performances. You'd think he would use her starring in her own show as a selling point, but instead the posters read: "Chelsea Handler from *Girls Behaving Badly* Live at Zanies This Weekend!"

I started to wonder if he knew about Chelsea's show.

Here is a stand-up poster that Rick sent to a Nashville comedy club. Chelsea Lately *had already been on the air a full year.*

Maybe he was like that guy from the movie *Memento* and he forgot new information within seconds of learning it. So I did everything I could to get Rick to update the information he used to promote Chelsea. This included hourly updated data on how her book was selling, organized breakdowns of her show's ratings, and bullet point lists of her most impressive credits. I even updated her Web site with new headshots and a short bio, so that all he had to do was send a link to club promoters. I FedEx'd over the scrapbooks I'd made, along with a new one I'd put together in private, after hours, when there was no chance Chelsea could walk in on me. I tried everything I could to help him make himself look like he had his shit together. He still never replied to me.

I was preparing myself for an all-out war with Rick when, out of nowhere, he started paying attention to me. Suddenly he was returning my calls, responding to my e-mails, and getting back to me via text message. *This is so great,* I thought. *He's finally taking me seriously as a businesswoman! He's recognizing the contributions I bring to the table and is finally coming around to my ideas! Mom was right. Hard work really does pay off!*

The sudden turn of events gave me an extra little skip in my step. The scoliosis that Chelsea had diagnosed me with disappeared, and I walked a little taller during this particular period of recognition.

Sadly, my newfound high came crashing down around me when I discovered that Chelsea had sneaked onto my computer and sent the following from my e-mail account.

From: Eva M.
Date: 6/14/2008
To: Rick
Hey Big Guy,
    What are you doing for lunch today? I'm
super duper horny and I'm just gonna say it:
my clit is burning for you. Can we meet?
    Ready and waiting,
    Eva

You see, Chelsea has tricked the world into believing that she is technologically retarded, but that's a lie. What I and several other victims have discovered is that she likes to sneak into people's work spaces, get on their computers without their knowledge, and wreak havoc. I don't know when she had the time to develop the computer skills she possesses. Maybe she takes night classes or is enrolled in online courses. If she is, I wish she'd tell me, because I'd like to frame her diploma when she graduates. Regardless, she's pretty shifty. She loves to send out random e-mails in your name. It's a known fact around the office: If you need to go to the bathroom, grab a bagel, or have a desire for a drink on Margarita Thursdays, you'd better remember to lock your computer before you leave. If you have a laptop it's better to just bring it with you. If you don't, Chelsea will humiliate you.

What's worse than the e-mails she sends to other people is the way you find out what she's done. Suddenly you start getting concerned voice mail messages from friends or family who are worried about your personal safety or your latest case of shingles.

When I found the e-mail that she'd sent to Rick, I was mortified. For the next six months, he insisted on communicating with me. He was suddenly adamant that we have face-to-face meetings. Although I was able to dodge a one-on-one dinner date, it was impossible not to run into him at Chelsea's stand-up shows. He'd follow me around all night and compliment my walk, while I smiled and nodded and pretended not to want to strangle him. Part of me was flattered; nobody had ever told me that I had a nice walk before, but once I remembered he wouldn't have been complimenting me if he didn't think my underwear was on fire for him, I'd get pissed off again. And yet, no matter how irritated I got, I just didn't have it in me to tell him that the e-mail had not been from me. I assumed he'd be more embarrassed than I was, especially once he recalled all of the times he had "accidentally" bumped into me with what I'm fairly certain was an erection.

Chelsea did nothing to help the situation. She knew that I was too terrified to confront Rick on his newfound creepiness, so she continued to egg him on. She would say things like "I think Eva has a crush on you..." to keep him interested. At one point Rick decided to tell Chelsea about the e-mail. Instead of coming clean, she played dumb.

"I can't say I'm surprised that she wrote that," Chelsea lied. "I think she really has it bad for you. She has some real horniness issues. She needs to unwind, and fucking is the only way she can do it."

To this day Rick and I have not cleared the air on the issue. I never told him the truth, and he never directly asked me about the e-mail. After a while I felt that too much time had passed and it was best to just let it go. I also figured that once he was no longer handling her personal appearances, I didn't have to worry about him handling anything personal of mine.

As I'm sure you can imagine, many of Chelsea's friends and family members are on high alert when they receive any e-mail that contains sensitive-sounding material. She's still able to fool most of us, but a few of the savvier people in her life have caught on to her. Her sister Simone is one of those people.

One afternoon I was searching through my e-mails for something I had sent to a club about one of Chelsea's upcoming shows when I noticed an e-mail that had been sent to Simone. Knowing that I hadn't e-mailed her that day, I felt instant panic. Great! What had "I" done this time? I opened the e-mail and read it.

From: Eva Magazine
To: Simone
Subject: Please Help Me
Hey Simone,

    I was just wondering if you could talk to Chelsea for me.

She's been really moody lately. I think she
is stressed out about something. I feel weird
telling you this, but she slapped me the other
day. I don't know how to approach her, and I'm
worried something worse is going on. I've never
been hit before. I wouldn't care if it was just
once, but obviously I don't want it to graduate
to a punch.

Please don't tell her I e-mailed you, I have
a wedding coming up and I don't want a black
eye.

Eva

Simone is a little more on top of things than Rick. Later
that day, I received this response.

From: Simone
To: Eva Magazine
Subject: RE: Please Help Me
Uh, you had me at hello..."graduate to a
punch?" Nice try, Chelsea.

Simone

P.S. Chels, it was a very solid effort (Shana
was ready to fly out and save Eva)

Even though Simone has become quick enough to
know when she is being Chelsea'd, a few others are still
learning.

Chelsea has a close friend and work colleague named Kevin. He and his partner, Brian, are two of Chelsea's longtime friends and by far some of the nicest people I have ever met. They are gracious, caring, giving, and

My adopted sisters (i.e., Chelsea's sisters Shoshanna and Simone) and me. Whether she likes it or not, Chelsea is a sister to me. We care and worry about each other, we will always be there for each other no matter what, and we know how to make each other nuts. I will be with her until we are old ladies, me and my Chelsea Handler–brand hearing aid.

nurturing. They've always been so good to me and I adore them. They are the kind of people who don't deserve to be fucked with. Unfortunately, Chelsea loves all of the people who are close to her equally. That means nobody gets special treatment...and nobody is safe. One afternoon I received this e-mail.

From: Kevin
To: Eva M.
Hi Eva,
    Good to hear from you. We'd love to have dinner this week. Can you come to our house on Tuesday around 7:30 PM? Delicious has offered to cook! Not a common occurrence. Ha ha. If not, we'll find another night.
    And don't worry; you can count on our complete discretion. We've both been there and understand how important your privacy is.
    Looking forward to it.

I had no idea what Kevin was talking about. I hadn't written to either of them in a while, so why would he be saying that it was "good to hear from" me? I know. Sometimes it still takes a few minutes for me to process the obvious. Once reality hit me, I went into my Sent folder to find out what kind of e-mail "I" had sent Kevin. My body went slightly numb when I found this.

From: Eva M.

To: Kevin

How are you? I was wondering if you and Brian
were free any nights this week to maybe grab
dinner at your place, and we could talk over a
couple of things. I've always admired a couple
that can make a same-sex partnership work and
would love to get your thoughts and/or advice
on that very topic. For now, I'd prefer to keep
this confidential, as I feel it is a sensitive
and challenging issue for me. I have not acted
on any of my sexual impulses yet, but I am
desperately yearning to and could really use
the insight that the two of you have. Please
let me know. Thanks so much!

I knew that Chelsea would be pretty pleased with
herself that Kevin had responded to me the way he had,
so I didn't tell her. I also knew that she would never come
to me and ask, so I figured I'd just let her sweat it out.
It was like putting a piece of steak outside a lion's cage
and watching the lion desperately try to find a way to get
to it. This was the only way I could give her any sort of
payback.

As the days passed, she was obviously getting impatient because, as I later found out, she took matters into
her own hands and decided to probe Kevin for a little
information.

From: CH

To: Kevin

I hear there's a secret lesbian coming over to the two big bears' house to confess her love of COSLOPI!!!!!!!!!!!!!!!!!!!!!! I am dying to know the details. Can I come over and eavesdrop? I could hide in a closet...just like Eva's been doing for years!

From: Kevin

To: CH

Hello, Chelsea.

Just as I would never divulge any of your confidences or betray your trust, I would appreciate you respecting the fact that I am also not at liberty to discuss anyone's personal life. If somebody wants to talk to you about something, then they will. In the meantime if they choose to talk to me, I must keep that in confidence. I hope you can respect that.

Love,

Kevin

Chelsea was dying. She flew into a fit of laughter and peed her pants at her desk. Yes, she does that often and, yes, it's disgusting. I cross my fingers that one day she'll have her bladder checked out. When she finally pulled herself together she decided that she should put an end to the joke. Kevin was obviously taking the whole thing very seriously, and she thought it was time to let him know it was all a big lie. At least that's what she told me; I think she just needed me to work that weekend and didn't want to lose me to a fake brunch.

From: CH

To: Kevin

Oh, really, dickhead? You want to respect her privacy? First you need to learn to respect my ability to fuck with you. Who do you think sent the e-mail in the first place?

P.S. Your response to her was nice. You're truly not a shitty person, but you're still gay and that will never change.

Kevin did not respond to Chelsea for three days. First he e-mailed me to confirm that he had been fucked with. Then he decided to give Chelsea the silent treatment, which he knew she couldn't stand. Chelsea knew that Kevin was trying to smoke her out, so she just waited idly by until he contacted her. That girl is made of steel.

Kevin finally decided to respond to her, knowing that she'd let this drag out as long as she needed to.

From: Kevin
To: CH
You're terrible, Muriel, just terrible. I want
to know one thing: What did your parents do
to you that turned you into such a crazed and
conniving lunatic? On top of that, how do you
have the time to send e-mails out from other
people's computers? Don't you have to tape a
television show every day? I usually tune in,
and while you do come off as unprepared and
butcher almost every person's name, I'd imagine
you put in at least a little bit of prep time.
Are you a fucking octopus?

From: CH
To: Kevin
I'm not an octopus, but I am an octoPUSSY. An
octoPUSSY that poor closeted Eva would really
like to get a hold of, but now she has no one
to talk to...

One thing Chelsea always is to her friends and her staff is generous. Perhaps it's her way of apologizing for, say, announcing your pregnancy to your family and throwing in your intention to raise your baby by yourself since the father could be any number of people.

One year Chelsea took her entire staff to Cabo San Lucas for her birthday. She also flew her family down to experience what was later referred to as the *"Chelsea Lately Gone Wild"* vacation in Mexico. For the record, Chelsea never called it that. In fact, she thinks most of us are stupid. She's kind of right: most people who work for her should abstain from alcohol.

Chelsea's family arrived together in Cabo. Leading the pack was her four-year-old niece, Charley. I hadn't met Charley yet and I was really excited to, because I'd heard so much about her. I bent down to her level, tried to ignore the pain in my lower spine, stuck out my hand, and said, "It's very nice to meet you, Ms. Charley. I've heard so much about you."

Charley looked at me and replied, "Am I supposed to know who you are?"

It was love at first insult. Any four-year-old who could give me shit was someone I definitely wanted to hang out with. That really goes for Chelsea's whole family. In fact, I'd go so far as to say that Chelsea has the world's greatest family. *My* family thinks that's rude to say, but most likely they won't be reading this, since they aren't super interested in what I do. All of Chelsea's brothers and sisters are funny and kind, and they've always been nothing but wonderful to me. I like to think of myself as their adopted sister, even though when I suggested this, they said that if they had the option to adopt me, they would not. Their family is big; I guess there isn't much room for one more.

For the rest of the Cabo trip I was attached at the hip to the Handlers. Well...every one of them except Chelsea's brother Roy. He had a strange way of interacting with me.

He was around me a lot, but I felt like he thought he had to be. Don't get me wrong; he was always nice, but most babysitters are. When he spoke to me, he addressed me as if I were a two-year-old. He would talk very slowly and then ask me if I understood.

"W-e'-r-e g-o-i-n-g t-o t-h-e p-o-o-l n-o-w, E-v-a. Do you want to get your bathing suit and come to the pool with us, Eva? Swimming is fun. Does Eva like swimming, too?"

I couldn't figure out if he was repeating my name for fear of forgetting it; I heard that some people use that as a memory trick. I also wasn't sure why he spoke so slowly, especially since I'd seen him interact with everybody else like a normal person. He even spoke to little Charley as if she were a grown woman. I have since recognized that Charley is a lot more mature than I am, but at the time, my feelings were hurt. Roy was always taking my hand and patting me on the back, saying, "G-o-o-d j-o-b," even if all I did was walk down a couple of steps.

On the last day in Cabo, Roy was nice enough to take me parasailing. He said that he'd heard I wanted to go, which I didn't, but I felt that it would have been rude to say no to his generous offer. I thought maybe he loved parasailing and was using me as an excuse to go. We headed to the beach. I noticed that Roy was carrying Charley's arm floaters and wondered if he was afraid of deep water. We got to the boat that was waiting to take us out into the ocean. Just as I started to board, Roy put his hand on my shoulder and stopped me.

"Shouldn't you take off your legs and leave them at the dock? The water is probably not good for the wood."

"What?" I asked, confused.

"Don't be scared. I brought arm floaties for extra safety," he said to me with a concerned look.

His odd behavior toward me suddenly made sense. Chelsea was busted. I made Roy spill the lie that Chelsea had told him about me. Prior to the Cabo trip, she had informed him that I was mentally disabled. As the story went, I was born in a Polish hospital and when I was delivered my umbilical cord was wrapped around my Polack neck. They were able to save me, but because of the amount of time I spent without air, I couldn't function at full capacity. The story didn't quite satisfy her, so she threw in that I had fake legs and loved water sports. Chelsea told Roy that she found out about my fake legs when I was on a trip with her in the Bahamas and wanted to go down a waterslide. According to her, I had to take my fake legs off and send them down the slide first.

Her story was so convincing that in order to prove to Roy that my legs were real I had to allow him to burn me with a cigarette. It wasn't until the tears started flowing that he was satisfied that my legs were made of my own flesh and blood.

Aside from my posture, Chelsea has always been very concerned with my sex life. Let me rephrase that: she has always been concerned about me and my lack of anything that remotely resembles what some might call a sex life.

I loved working for Chelsea and wanted to stay focused.

Brad, Roy, and me heading to Cabo. You can see my leg naturally goes in different directions from my body. I believe Chelsea saw this and capitalized on it.

Hamlet

Having a guy to worry about was the last thing I needed. Word on the street was that Hamlet, the security guard, liked me, so at least I had *something* going.

One night I stayed late to organize Chelsea's nail polish colors. She walked into the office and I proudly whipped open her makeup drawer.

"Ta-da!" I exclaimed with pride. "Looks like *somebody's* manicures will be operating with a new level of professional efficiency!"

Chelsea stopped, looked at the drawer, and then looked at me. "This looks like the work of someone who needs to get laid," she said and then walked out.

From that point on she became relentless, pitching me to any and all male candidates. If you were a heterosexual male and came to our office anytime during the fall of 2009, Chelsea asked you to have sex with me. She was always on the lookout. Crew guys, bartenders, busboys—you name 'em, she offered me up to them. Still, I was a big disappointment to her; I was always too busy rearranging her bookshelves and secretly scrapbooking to focus on my own sexual needs.

One night, during a stop in Austin on Chelsea's "Bang Bang" tour, she was having dinner with her friend Johnny and her opener, Jo Koy. I had passed on the meal and opted to stay in the hotel room and color-code the clothes in Chelsea's suitcase. Jo asked why I hadn't joined them for dinner, and a light bulb went off in Chelsea's head.

"Oh, she can't sit still long enough to eat a full meal. Eva gets super horny on the road," she told Jo.

Johnny has been around Chelsea long enough to know the game, so he chimed in immediately. "Yeah, I banged her a couple of times in San Jose," he added.

Jo was really confused. He and I had known each other for a really long time. We went way back, to when he used to do stand-up at the Denver club I worked in. He didn't think this sounded like me at all. In fact, he thought I was kind of standoffish.

"Really?" Jo asked. "She doesn't seem like she sleeps around like that."

"Oh, yeah, that's her thing," Chelsea told him. "She acts like she's a good girl, but she porks everybody. It gets worse when we're on the road. I think it has something to do with hotels and something that went down when she was in elementary school. Eva is pretty wound up, and sex is the only thing that seems to take the edge off for her."

"That's really surprising. I thought she was uptight." Jo still couldn't wrap his head around the new information.

"She used to be uptight, until she started doing anal," Chelsea fired back.

Chelsea and Johnny continued to tell Jo Koy all about my sexual escapades. Chelsea told him that I had pretty much had sex with everybody at the office. She said that sometimes Chris Franjola took a turn. If Chris was too wiped out from meeting up with girls on Facebook, then Ian the PA took care of my needs. Chelsea explained to Jo that she wasn't really an advocate of my behavior, but that I obviously had some sort of medical condition and sex was

221

the only way I could be satiated. After all, I worked for her now, and she wanted what was best for her employees. If constant porking was what kept me alert, then constant porking it would be. She also told him that I had even gone so far as to sleep with Jeremy, the guy at the office who everyone was certain had never taken a shower.

Here's where the story takes a twist that even Chelsea couldn't have anticipated: Jo Koy and I had just started dating at the time. I hadn't had the chance to tell Chelsea about it yet; it was pretty new. Honestly, I was avoiding telling her. That turned out to be a big mistake, because it turns out that she actually encourages inter-office romance. Jo was texting me throughout the entire dinner, but was not mentioning any of the things Chelsea was saying to him. He was obviously afraid to rattle my cage, for fear that one mean text from him would send me into a fury and I'd screw the bellhop.

Later that night, he called me and grilled me about my supposed sexual disorder.

"Really? Jeremy? That guy probably hasn't bathed in six months! Last time I saw him he had nacho cheese in his beard and when I asked him about it he said he hadn't had nachos in three weeks!"

"Have you ever been tested? Do I need to get tested?" Jo was concerned.

It took me a while to understand what he was upset about and even longer to calm him down. After four hours of talking, he finally understood that he was just another victim of a lie that Chelsea Handler had told.

It's hard to find a way to get back at Chelsea for the pranks she's pulled. Every time anyone has tried they've failed. She's too smart to fall for it, so you really have to go behind her back and through other channels.

It's no secret that Chelsea and her dad have a love/hate relationship. He has asked her for money on more than one occasion, even though he has plenty of his own. He assumes that now that she's making money she should be taking care of him. The way the two of them communicate completely stresses me out, because I just want everything with her family to be fine. So I came up with the idea to mend fences for her. If it also resulted in a little bit of pay-back, then I'd consider that a bonus.

One day Chelsea received a phone call from one of her sisters letting her know how much their father appreciated the beautiful letter Chelsea had sent him. When Chelsea asked what letter she was talking about, her sister read it to her:

Dear Daddy,

I am so sorry that we have had any arguments over the past couple of years about money or about anything else. I've really been thinking about things and I have come to realize that you're right. I am now in a position to support you financially. The fact that you have enough money to support yourself and your cleaning lady doesn't matter. You brought me into this world and as a thank-you I should be there to see you out of it. You are an amazing man, regardless of what any of the past renters of our home in Martha's Vineyard have said. From now on what's mine is yours! I can't wait to see you next Christmas. Maybe we can go sledding, LOL!

—Chelsea

Chelsea instantly knew that the letter was written by me. She told her sister that nobody else would talk like that except Eva. "Doesn't he recognize his own daughter's handwriting?" she asked.

"It was typed," Shana explained.

Chelsea sent me a text that read, *Nice one.* That was the only reaction she gave me. I actually think the whole thing made her want to promote me, and she might have, if there had been a position to promote me to.

I was glad the letter got a bit of a response from her, but it just proved to me that when it comes to pranks, Chelsea Handler can't be beat. Even though Jo now knows the truth about my sex life, part of what Chelsea said stuck in his head. Every once in a while, when I don't answer my phone, he thinks I'm at a homeless shelter picking out my next sex partner. Kevin and Brian still try to offer to let me "meet up" with one of their single lesbian friends. On top of that, Chelsea's brother Roy still treats me like I'm mildly retarded. Last time I was at Chelsea's pool, he handed me two inflatable arm bands and a rubber duckie and suggested I stay in the shallow end.

For the record: I am still not positive that Eva's legs are made from real human parts, or that Eva herself is even human. She is a very strange duck, and her posture leaves a lot of room for improvement. She is a better person than I am, but that doesn't really mean much. She is also a better daughter to my father than I am, but my father has sex on a regular basis with his cleaning lady. I would also like to point out that up until I met Eva, she wore blue eye shadow on her lids.

—Chelsea

This photo sums up my relationship with Eva perfectly. I look on with confusion when I see a boat headed straight for us in the Bahamas, as Eva smiles like a lunatic.

225

Chapter Ten

Lies and Other Things
I Wish Were Lies

AMY MEYER

LIES

I would never lie; I willfully participate in a campaign of misinformation.

—FOX MULDER

Me; my mom, Kris; and Chelsea before her show in Kansas City.

I have known Chelsea, or "Handy," for over four years, and it is no surprise to me that I was asked to weave a tale of her creative and sordid lies. Don't get me wrong. Handy is sweet, generous, and loyal to a fault, but she *loves* to lie. Her delight over lying is woven through with a sweet slice of sadism. We love her without exactly knowing why. Well, on second thought, we could always chalk it up to Stockholm syndrome.

Being Chelsea's stylist has afforded me the opportunity to be privy to many intimate moments of her life. Here are some that she has agreed to let me print.

Chelsea loved to lie to her ex-boyfriend Ted. I actually believe his sweet and loyal gullibility is the reason their relationship was extended by six months.

On more than one occasion, while Chelsea was getting her hair done for the show, I watched her pick up the phone, call Ted, and tell him that she had fallen down the stairs and broken her collarbone, lost hearing in one or both ears, or was pregnant with his child. On one occasion I witnessed her say she was pregnant while she had a margarita and cigarette in hand. Time and time again, Ted believed her; he believed the woman he was madly in love with was carrying his child. Why would anyone lie about that? Because they are a sick fuck, that's why. Although if Chelsea ever carried a baby to full term, she would be a wonderful mother. Not only is she compassionate and protective, she incessantly spoils the ones she loves (in between lying to them).

Each time she attempted to convince Ted that he was going to be a silver-haired daddy, she would up the ante. On her initial attempt she was very serious and stressed out.

"Ted, I'm late. I just took a pregnancy test and it came out positive. I can't even think straight, my hormones are all out of whack, and...I just ate Taco Bell for lunch. There has got to be a baby inside me."

When Ted responded, "Everything is going to be okay, honey. I love you, and we will figure this out together," she replied, "You are so ridiculous," and hung up the phone.

The second and third time went something like this: Chelsea crying, "Ted, I'm pregnant and I'm not kidding. None of my clothes fit. I think I'm already showing."

In Ted's typical problem-solving style, he suggested she wear Spanx, to which she barked, "Ted, that will give the baby brain damage. I don't want the baby to be slow. We already have Chuy."

Why, I'm sure you're asking yourself, would Ted have believed these shenanigans? Because Chelsea is infectious. She can be so warm and fun that you want to believe her just to be part of her world. I'm here to tell you that that world is overrated.

A favorite Ted lie of mine, and one that I think is so telling of their relationship, is the "very, very, very, superior Chelsea" lie. This happened on a Tuesday night. It was just the two of them, so I'm assuming her ADD ass was in high gear and she was bored out of her mind.

They were having dinner at some fancy restaurant and Chelsea said, "Oh, so I got the results back from my IQ test today. I scored a hundred and fifty. Is that good?"

I can only presume this line was delivered in complete seriousness and as an aside, right before ordering some albacore sashimi. Like, "Yeah, Albert Einstein's IQ was one-sixty and I'm Chelsea Handler cruising through the west side of Los Angeles with my very superior IQ of one-fifty. It ain't no thang."

There are so many responses you can imagine or hope that a boyfriend would have upon hearing that his girlfriend is another Einstein. But one wouldn't expect him to put his head in his hands and, after a long beat of silence, say, "I was afraid of something like this."

The revelation of Chelsea's genius IQ completely changed the dynamic of their relationship. Ted is a very smart and capable man—he was the CEO of our company at the time—and had the wherewithal to bag Chelsea Handler, but make no mistake about it: Ted is *not* a genius. From that moment on, there was no denying that she now had the upper hand in the relationship. (Technically, this would make Ted the "bottom.") If they ever argued over the show or even about restaurant choices, all she had to say was "I'm sorry, which one of us is the genius?"

Chelsea Handler is a sharp cookie and has a beautifully

bizarre brain. She may also be many things, but she is *not* a genius.

To be honest, I have no idea how many times Chelsea has lied to me. Most likely it's already occurred at least twice this morning.

During our first season on air, she and our executive producer, Tom, told me that we were going to hang Chuy on the cross for the Christmas episode. The art department was building a cross, and I had one day to pull together a Jesus costume. Tom and Chelsea let me know it was really important to make the costume look authentic. If we were going to piss off the Christians, it had to be done right.

"No problem," I assured them. I already had the muslin cloth to make Chuy's loincloth. Warner Bros.' costume department had the rope sandals we needed for Chuy's nugget feet. All I had to do was make a crown of thorns. "Oh and how bloody do you want to make him?" I asked.

"Amy, the man was nailed to a cross," Chelsea told me. "It wasn't a pretty situation. But this *is* Christmas, so find a happy middle ground."

The next day Chelsea was in her makeup chair when I paraded Jesus Chuy in for her approval. If you can make Chelsea laugh, it's a pretty good feeling, even if you don't realize that she's laughing at you.

"Oh, my God, Amy, get Tom down here!" she howled, holding her vagina as she's known to do when she's comedically aroused. Seconds later, Tom appeared in Chelsea's office and fell into hysterics. I felt amazing. Then Chelsea instructed Chuy to practice the line "Fuck the Jews!"

"Fuck the Yews," Chuy exclaimed. "Fuck the Yews!"

I was horrified. "We are not going to have him say, 'Fuck the Jews,' Chelsea, are we?"

She was now searching through her underwear drawer while holding her vagina, looking for a fresh pair to replace the ones she had clearly soiled.

"Chelsea, are we really going to have him say that?"

"No! Amy! No, we aren't doing any of this," she said, rolling around on the floor with her legs in the air. "Do you think the network would ever let us dress him as a bloody Jesus and yell, 'Fuck the...'" She couldn't get it out. Her laughter had turned silent; she wasn't making a noise, but her shoulders were shaking. "I have to say," she managed to get out after a few moments, "you did an amazing job on that outfit." Then she stood up, with fresh panties in hand, wiped the tears from her face, and headed to the bathroom. "He looks amazing. But, seriously, take it off. We have a show to do."

Let me clarify. I'm not stupid, but Handy gets me time and time again. In exchange for my hard work, Chelsea had allowed me to swaddle Chuy and place him in a manger. Later that day, she left an envelope with a thousand dollars in cash on my desk, with a note that said, "I appreciate your dedication to your craft, even though you're very stupid."

Chelsea and me lying in bed in New York City the day
Chelsea Chelsea Bang Bang *came out.*

THINGS THAT I WISH WERE LIES

As her stylist, I see Chelsea naked on a regular basis. That's pretty intimate, so I try to maintain a professional atmosphere during fittings. "What-the-fuck-ever" is usually what I'm met with.

While getting her dressed—which, I might add is my job—all of the following things have happened to me. (Please keep in mind that I was working during these experiences.)

232

- She smacked me in the face with her tits.
- Burping in my face? Done.
- Once, while standing in front of the mirror butt-ass naked, she said, "Hey, Amy, look at this piece of left-over toilet paper." I had already turned my head and looked at what she was pointing at before I realized what she was saying.
- When I first started working with her, I wore dresses and skirts all the time. Because she likes to expose her staff's genitalia, I now wear underwear and pants.
- I was introduced as her big lesbian stylist in person and on national television.
- Peeing in front of me? Those were the days.
- She has trimmed her fifteen pubic hairs in my presence. At this point in our relationship, I think some mystery could be a good thing.

One of the perks of my fabulous and fun job is that I get to travel with Chelsea. My responsibilities on the road are a cross between those of butler and camp counselor. I pack her, unpack her, lay out her clothes, and make sure the group gets where we are going on time and that no one is left behind when we are drunk. The upside to catering to Chelsea's every need is that I get to travel all over the world with my friends while laughing my ass off. And we always get to stay at fabulous hotels. The downside is the following:

Every night before bed, Chelsea orders a movie.

Sometimes the films she chooses are great. Usually they are not. She inevitably falls asleep within the first fifteen minutes of the flick. Sometimes I do, too. Which is why we have watched *Eat Pray Love* three times. We have yet to experience "Love." Sometimes the shitty movies get me hooked and I can't fall asleep until Tom Cruise has saved someone.

Like Chelsea, I am a Pisces, which makes for a sensitive and empathetic person. I can't watch movies in which people have fucked-up lives or have fucked up their lives. I can't watch scary or traumatic movies, either. After one Saturday night of partying, Chelsea made Johnny Kansas and me get into bed with her and we ordered *Precious*. We both protested her choice. She insisted there were some very funny scenes with Mariah Carey, and that the movie was actually a dark comedy. We gave in. Handy fell asleep within minutes, while Johnny and I both had nightmares for weeks.

Chelsea loves to say really inappropriate things to people. She does this with a smile on her face and in a very sweet voice that is low enough to hear but that makes you think you may have heard wrong. This practice of hers never fails to mortify me. It makes me extremely uncomfortable. Here are some real-life examples:

An African American bellhop walked into our hotel room to collect our bags. Chelsea walked out of the bathroom and smiled at him. He smiled back and said, "Good morning, Miss Handler. I hope you're enjoying your stay with us." She replied, "Yes, I am. Thank you." As he turned his back to place our bags on the luggage cart, she said in a sweet, soft voice intended only for my ears, "Wanna show me your big black cock?" Halfway through the word *cock*, I exclaimed in a loud and authoritative voice, "And these bags need to go, too, sir. What a beautiful day it is here in sunny Baltimore!" I did not shut up until he'd walked out the door with a fifty-dollar tip.

After MTV's Video Music Awards, Chelsea took Gina (hair and makeup), all the writers, and me to Cabo to thank us for doing both the VMA and *Chelsea Lately* simultaneously. Chelsea wanted all of us to really relax, so she had her assistant set up a day at the spa for us. What a sweet boss. We get to the spa, check in, and our host takes us girls to the women's locker room for a tour. Obviously Spanish was this woman's first language, but she was speaking English, so I assumed she could understand it. As she was showing us the showers, Chelsea smiled and sweetly said, "Thanks. Do you take it up the tushie? My girlfriend here loves it in the anal cavity." Our host showed us the steam room, and Chelsea responded with "Great. I'll bet you have a very hairy pussy." Next we were shown where to place our robes and dirty towels. Chelsea asked, "Wanna show me your pretty pussy?" The woman smiled through all of this, but I swear she was looking at us like we were nuts. Needless to say, I separated from the group as fast as possible. All of us are horrified when Chelsea does stuff like this, but the amazing thing is no one ever really seems to hear her except us. Her sisters have told me she has been pulling the under-her-breath shit for years, and that as long as she does it with a big smile on her face, the victim can never quite accept what he's heard.

Once, Chelsea shot a movie in Vancouver with Reese Witherspoon (cool, chic, smart, funny: we adore her). One day we wrapped early. We decided to head back to our room, order room service, watch movies, and take a Lunesta so we could fall asleep at 9:30 PM. Dream evening! What a treat! Then the room service guy arrived. We had ordered a ton of shit and wanted to eat in bed. It's the Four Seasons. The service is always impeccable, and this evening was no exception. Our server laid place mats on our bed, arranging our five-star dining experience.

Here is a sample of what came from Chelsea's mouth while he was doing so: "Hi, sir, do you want to have a little fucky time with me? How big is your penis? I adore getting my pussy licked." As she was saying all of these things, I scrambled out of the bed and shuffled him into the living room to place our food there. I had to tell him where to place everything, in an attempt to shut out Chelsea's voice. When he placed a plate of French fries in front of her, she said in a loud voice, "Thank you, sir. That is very funny-looking spaghetti." I looked at her and grabbed her face, and my eyes were saying, "Shut the fuck up" as my mouth said in a loud and slow voice, "No, Chelsea, these are French fries!" Then I signed the check, and that guy got the fuck out of our room as fast as he could move. Once the door shut, Chelsea jumped out of the bed laughing and holding her vagina so she wouldn't pee in her underwear. For three days she would reenact my saying "No, Chelsea, these are French fries!" like I was Forrest Gump, and then laugh uncontrollably. The girl loves to laugh, especially when no one else is laughing with her.

Everyone in Chelsea's life is there for two reasons: she loves them, and they are willing to be humiliated.

Chelsea did a stand-up show in Tampa with Jo Koy. After they performed, everyone in Handy's entourage— her agent; her assistant, Eva; her brother Roy; her tour manager, Michelle; and I—retreated to our suite to kick it. When room service arrived, Chelsea asked our server if she wanted to "show us her pussy." The server looked up from the tray of food and said, "I don't think so, Chelsea. I'm familiar with your program." Game over.

This is a formal apology to everyone we have encountered and to those we are yet to meet. I apologize. Chelsea is a really good person, but she is sick and can't help herself.

E IS FOR EXCEDRIN

Once, on a Monday (TRUE FUCKING STORY) I picked up an Excedrin bottle, took two pills, put them in my mouth, and swallowed. I had a horrible headache. Chelsea had a really busy day: a show taping, followed by a post-tape interview, followed by a meeting in Tom's office with her agents, followed by a fitting to get her dressed so she could dash out the door and go to a red carpet event. No room for fuck-ups. Period.

An hour before I dressed Chelsea for the show, I started to feel weird. Waves of nausea began to roll through me. I was unable to focus on the type on my computer screen. Something was seriously wrong with me. A chemical reaction was occurring in my body. I decided that I must be diabetic and was headed for a diabetic coma. It also crossed my mind that this was karma for dressing up the guys from the show as the Jonas Brothers for a skit where we talked about Kevin Jonas having diabetes: type 2.

I told my assistant, Linda, that after the last fitting, she was going to have to take me to the emergency room. In the meantime she was not allowed to leave my side. Linda was not amused. She was looking at me as if I were crazy. I was. Instead of a chair at my desk, I have one of those large workout balls. For an hour I sat on it bouncing and shopping for shoes on the Barneys Web site, while telling Linda and the production assistants that I hoped I wasn't dying. Chelsea walked by and asked if we had some sexy dresses for an event. I said, "Totally!" After she was gone I turned to Linda and said, "What are we going to do?" She replied, "Dress her, Amy. Like we do every day?" and looked at me as if I were bat-shit crazy.

Let's take a second to discuss Linda, my amazing Vietnamese American assistant. She is the consummate professional. I am the creative force of our department, but she helps legitimize my professional existence. Linda stands at about five feet, two inches tall, and she has a perfectly round, beautiful Vietnamese face. When she started working on our show, she was a little on the thick side. Chelsea nicknamed her Paccy, as in Ms Pac Man. Anytime Linda walked into Chelsea's office, Chelsea would say, "Wocca wocca wocca!" Everyone in our office still calls her Paccy, except me. I call her Shorty.

Chelsea still texts Linda from time to time to ask how many ghosts she caught over the weekend, and what her high score is. She will also ask her, in complete seriousness, if it's hard for her to get down the stairs with no legs. After I informed Chelsea that Linda had hired a trainer and lost twenty pounds because of her nickname, Chelsea was appalled at her own behavior. She had no idea that nicknaming her Paccy would have any sort of negative impact on Pacc. Instead of apologizing, Chelsea bought Paccy her very own Ms Pac Man machine and had it delivered to Linda's parents' house, where she will reside until marriage. The note read, "This is for all the nights you are stuck at home living with your parents in the seventeenth century, while you could be out wocca wocca-ing your coslopus. P.S. I liked you better with a little meat on you."

Dressing Chelsea is fun, but it is not always easy. Never mind the distraction of e-mails and Twitters she constantly gets from fans informing her that her stylist must hate her. She does not like to try on clothes. There are better things she could be doing with her time. Bitch is busy. With her, you get one or two shots. Precision is key, and when it is hard to focus on objects in front of you, as it was for me that Monday when I took the Excedrin, precise you are not. If it were not for my assistant I'm not sure Chelsea would have been dressed that day.

Chelsea asked me what pants she needed to wear with the top I handed her. My reply: "What do you feel like, slacks or jeans?" She looked at me like I was crazy.

"Really, Amy? Slacks? Is this an episode of *Mad Men?*"

There are three words Chelsea never likes to hear: moist, hose, and slacks.

Linda, who is an angel, handed me a pair of slacks and said, "These are the *pants* you picked out to go with that top, and here are the red heels you wanted."

Handy was reading her show notes while we put the finishing touches on her, so she did not notice that I was melting down in my own personal universe.

Linda and I went back to the wardrobe room, and I told her I would not be able to leave. Paccy would have to be on set. Something really bad was happening to me. Possibly death. This was not the time to discuss the budget with Gary, the line producer, and there was no way I was going to have a conversation with Chelsea. She may not be a genius, but she was too fucking smart to talk to my retarded ass at that point. Let's just say that I was barely holding it together.

By the grace of God, and the comedy of Chelsea, we got her through the first episode, then the post-tape interview, and then she was off to her meeting. By now a few other people in the office had noticed that something was wrong with me. Turkey, an intern Chelsea had nicknamed due to her body type, turned to the makeup girl and said, "Amy is acting like she is on mushrooms."

While I was racing to put out all the jewelry, shoes, and clothes for the last fitting, I was totally freaking out. Linda was getting really annoyed with me at this point, but I didn't care. This was life and death. My only hope was that this fitting would go well so I could get to the hospital before going into a diabetic coma. Linda and I went over our top-five dress choices and which shoes would go with which bags.

Chelsea breezed into her office, looked through the rack of dresses, and picked her favorite. My mouth was shut as I, holding my breath, zipped her in. It fit like a glove. She loved it. The shoes Linda placed on her feet were met with approval. She checked herself out in the mirror and told us, "Well, for once, I don't look ridiculous," and then turned on her heel and ran to the editing bay to watch a field piece before heading out the door.

I left Linda in Handy's room to clean up while I retreated to the bathroom in an attempt to collect myself and calm down. As I was splashing my face with cold water, I looked in the mirror and noticed that my pupils were the size of saucers. Proof! Something was really fucked up with me. My chemical balance was off. All day, fucking Linda had been treating me like I was a nut, BUT I WAS NOT! I really might die. Yet I had been able to stay and dress Chelsea three different times. Best employee ever.

Turkey and a coworker were outside the bathroom as I rushed out. "You guys, something is totally wrong with me. Look at my pupils. I think I'm about to sink into a coma."

They both looked at me as if I were a madwoman. Turkey responded, "Walk me through your day."

"Okay. I shopped this morning, and dropped off some clothes at Chelsea's house. I had a horrible headache so I took two Excedrin." My coworker stopped me and asked where I'd gotten the bottle of Excedrin. I told them, "In Chelsea's bedroom."

Long pause. With huge smiles, they informed me that I was rolling my fucking face off. Ecstasy was in that bottle.

You have got to be shitting me. How could I have been so stupid? All the signs were there. Oh yeah, it was noon on a Monday. I didn't think Ecstasy was in the game plan.

Armed with the knowledge that I would be dancing for the next eight hours, I retreated to the couch in Chelsea's room, where I started trying on her shoes. She and I share the same shoe size, which comes in handy about twice a week. Linda walked in, looked at me, and rolled her eyes.

"Um, listen up, little snooty assistant," I told her. "I'm not crazy. I accidentally took two hits of Ecstasy, so you don't have to take me to the emergency room."

Linda has never done drugs in her life. Not once. She goes to church on Sundays. So this news floored her. Then Chelsea walked in the room, was informed of the situation at hand, and didn't miss a beat as she proceeded to make me a cocktail.

Once I figured out what the fuck my Monday had turned into, I had an amazing evening. Thank God for Ms Pac Man.

A VERY BLURRY LINE

We spend a lot of time in Mexico. We like the sun, tequila, and fish tacos. Chelsea loves to spend at least one day at sea on a yacht. Lucky for us she always takes an interesting group of friends along for the ride. Not so lucky for me, on one of these glamorous days she peed on me.

This is me on that day on the boat,
pre-urination.

243

I was sunbathing on the front deck, when Handy came and got me. She said, "Amy, I want to show you something."

We went to the back of the boat and she told me to sit in the captain's fishing chair. She climbed up with me and said, "I just wanted to share this beautiful view with you. We are so lucky that we get to live this amazing life and I'm so glad that I get to share it with you." As she spoke these lovely words, she urinated on me.

That pretty much sums up our beautiful and weird friendship.

This is me contemplating when my life took a wrong turn, post-urination.

I would like to take this opportunity to say that I would only ever urinate on someone I truly adored, and I would only do it pool- or seaside, so we could immediately rinse off...together. When all is said and done, it is a bonding experience, and there is only a handful of people who can say they have been urinated on by me. I take my urination very seriously and am selective about whom I share it with. I also promise never to take it any further than that. Shadoobies are off limits.

I believe the real question here is who are all these people who continue to be friends with me after they've been peed on?

—Chelsea

Chapter Eleven

Pubescent and Adolescent Mendacity, 1985–1991

GLEN HANDLER

Chelsea has three older brothers, of whom I'm the youngest.

In the summer of 1974, my parents told me they were "thinking" about having another baby. This was alarming news to me. I was a serious ten-year-old boy and I strongly advised my parents against this idea, because it was clear there were already way too many people in the family, and none of them seemed particularly solvent. My parents smiled politely at my counsel, and my mother, Rita, offered some soothing words of encouragement about how much I'd enjoy another sister or brother, since I had been so helpful and supportive with baby Shoshanna.

Easy for her to say, since it became obvious later that she was already three months knocked up, had no relationship

*1979, Chelsea on my shoulders in Martha's Vineyard with
Simone, Shana, and our family friend Sam Gaidemak.*

with birth control, and was not "thinking" about having
another baby; she was *having* one. Since I was eleven years
old when Chelsea was born, I helped raise her with my
mom. My father (aka Platypus) never changed her diaper.

Growing up with five much older siblings made Chelsea older through osmosis. She also was forced to think for
herself, since no one in our family provided guidance of any
kind. Don't get me wrong. Our family was very loving and
nurturing; we just were not in the business of offering one
another meaningful counsel on how to navigate the world.
Our upbringing was a very comforting, warm, and direc-
tionless love-in, but any efforts involving parental guidance

and/or social interaction outside the four walls of the house were nonstarters. If you wanted a ride somewhere, to sign up for Little League, or your parents to go to the parent-teacher conference, you were completely out of luck, unless you assumed the role of the parent and became your own parent. So that's what we did. We were child adults.

Not surprisingly, it was clear early on that Chelsea was advanced beyond her age in terms of sensibility and wit and that she enjoyed the attention of others, especially older people, while simultaneously barely tolerating those in her own age group. Her older-than-her-years outlook shaped her entire existence. It basically allowed her to skip the long parts of childhood that are a complete waste of time, such as art and music class and the Girl Scouts, and concentrate on the more interesting parts of life, such as why most people are so hopelessly fucked up in the head.

Chelsea was six when I left for college at age seventeen, and ten when I graduated at age twenty-one. She visited me at college with the rest of my family and was a little too comfortable hanging out with me and my fraternity brothers at the AEPi fraternity house at Emory University, in Atlanta. It's always reassuring when your ten-year-old sister very easily flirts with your twenty-one-year-old fraternity brothers, who themselves act as if she's just a fellow co-ed. It's even more reassuring when the gaping age difference completely vaporizes the second your sister starts butchering your frat brothers' hair, clothes, faces, and witless comebacks.

"You know she's ten years old," I'd occasionally remind my lecherous university comrades.

"I know, Glen, but I could really see myself going out with her," said more than one frat brother.

"That's great, guys," I said. "Statutory rape has always been underrated."

I moved back home after college, since my first job was with a CPA firm half a mile from my house. It was a fun place to work. It was full of weirdos, and was not too uptight as workplaces go. There was the usual collection of social misfits who formed the melting pot of mid-1980s New Jersey—lots of Jewish, Italian, and Irish accountants debating the dreadful merits of debits, credits, balance sheet adjustments, and deferred income taxes. Fortunately, most folks had a decent sense of humor, except for one or two born-again Christians and one or two complete pricks.

At this firm, one was required to work Tuesday and Thursday nights and Saturdays during the busy so-called "tax season." The company provided dinner, so the accountants could quickly get back to churning out tax returns. These extra hours were somewhat flexible and not strictly enforced, so I always went home after the day shift ended, since home was just up the block. I would eat my mother's cooking, get rid of my suit and tie, and come back in a more reasonable wardrobe: jeans and a T-shirt. Sometimes I would take a nap and come back to work kind of late.

I started bringing then-twelve-year-old Chelsea to the office on those nights, most likely because there certainly was nothing for her to do at home and because I thought she was the perfect party favor for a wretched evening of tax-related drudgery. Naturally she was a huge hit at the office, and she loved it because there was no real supervision, since the partners didn't work late. She had an instant large audience of mutant adult accountants to insult, and there was free Coca-Cola, which we would eventually wind up stealing by the caseload when we expanded our visits to even more oddball hours.

Chelsea didn't exactly befriend people as much as steal coins from their desks, insult the introverts and the socially awkward, and entertain anyone whom she wasn't insulting. Typical of the conversations she had with the staff were the following:

CLOSETED HOMOSEXUAL AND AWKWARD ACCOUNTANT STAN ISAACSON (after being introduced to Chelsea): Well, it was nice meeting you.

CHELSEA: I wish I could say the same... Why would you ever choose to be an accountant?

SI: It's what I do best and I enjoy it... Why are you so obnoxious?

CHELSEA: It's what I do best and I enjoy it... Now, moving along, did you dress yourself this morning or did your mother pick out your clothes, because you look ridiculous.

SI: Glen, what's up with your dick of a sister?

CHELSEA: Oh, did I hurt your feelings?

SI: I don't have to put up with this nonsense.
CHELSEA: No, you don't . . . but you will and you'll enjoy it.
SI: Get your little sister out of here, Glen.

These encounters were par for the course and they went on ad infinitum. It was a pleasure. Chelsea used the CPA office as a sort of tree house escape from our regular house. Inexplicably, no one really questioned why an overly developed teenage girl was there during working hours, and most of my coworkers got used to her presence.

On a few occasions, when I worked alone past midnight and long after everyone else had left, Chelsea would pass out on an empty couch in a partner's office, presumably after stealing all of the desk change first. Sometimes she would leave early without telling me and walk the half mile back home alone. Sometimes, not realizing she was passed out on one of the couches, I would leave without her. That was a small problem, because one time she accidentally activated the security alarm when she tried to escape the locked office and ran back to the house in full criminal mode. Fun stuff, especially when you're a twelve-year-old girl.

When I worked late and nobody else was there, Chelsea would walk around the office making phone calls to friends and family from people's desks. Sometimes my work buddies knew Chelsea was there and they'd call in just to talk to her. Stan the homosexual had no personal life and he would often call in to speak to Chelsea in a lame attempt to psychoanalyze her. Chelsea would proceed to psychoanalyze him and tell him to get a fucking life. They would then proceed to give each other the silent treatment over the phone for about thirty minutes before one of them hung up. Deranged? Certainly, but refreshing nevertheless. Stan still talks about those phone calls.

I was particularly friendly with coworkers Marco, Mitch, and Ross, since we all were in our early twenties and liked to drink, smoke pot, and try to meet girls on the weekends. In fact, there were plenty of other twentysomething aspiring accountants in the company and they all joined in on the frivolity; it was more or less like one big happy fraternity. Most of us played on the company softball team together and got drunk afterward, and went to the same big alcohol-cocaine-pot-fueled house parties and got absolutely wasted. Chelsea would sometimes accompany me to those parties. Hey, why *not* let your underage high school sister tag along for some wholesome fun?

Obviously I wasn't the most responsible brother Chelsea could have had, but it would be too much for me to shoulder the blame for her errant behavior. She was going to do what she wanted. She was on a mission, and that mission was to party and meet men.

Chelsea spent several summers with her insane girlfriend Karen rampaging through the house party scene on the island playground that is Martha's Vineyard. I don't know exactly what they did, except that they were always cheerfully drunk and slept very late. They worked as waitresses at the local restaurants; in exchange for good customer service,

Chelsea at a teenage beauty pageant.
She was fourteen in this picture.

they managed to systematically ingratiate themselves with their customers for the specific purpose of being invited to all the alcohol-fueled house parties that might be occurring anywhere on the Vineyard. In spite of their very teenage DNA, they somehow came off as legitimate, albeit somewhat fermented, twenty-two-year-old women who were trying and wildly succeeding at having a good fucking time.

My mother and father had essentially abandoned any further parental supervision, since that was the equivalent of trying to paint the ocean; it couldn't be done and it had never worked and they were tired anyway. Besides, our mother, Rita, was busy most of the time reading nine-hundred-page books and befriending strangers she met at the A&P. The best strategy for raising Chelsea was to hope for no disasters while endlessly shaking your head in disbelief at her daily encounters with the neighborhood watch, at the confused victims of her prolific storytelling, at Karen's German shepherd's psychological and self-esteem issues, and at Chelsea's run-ins with Carly Simon.

In spite of Chelsea's completely adult lifestyle, my parents had persuaded her that she needed to continue with high school. Chelsea halfheartedly agreed, but she was violently opposed to returning to Livingston High School in New Jersey, since she felt that the student-teacher-asshole ratio, combined with the demanding structure of actually attending standard classes, was unacceptable and outrageous. Fortunately, my parents were able to enroll her for the next two years at the Livingston Alternative School, which of course was a wayward public school program for the disabled, unmotivated, agoraphobic, triskaidekaphobic, and/or those students who were unusually high on marijuana.

Chelsea flourished at the Alternative School because absolutely nothing was expected of the students there. Self-study was the prescribed teaching plan; this entailed reading books of your own choice and talking about them later whenever the hell you felt like it. Homework didn't exist, teacher interaction was like camp counselor interaction, and attendance was not viewed as an indicator of achievement. Lunch was served, but only after most students got high together. There were only a small number of students at the Alternative School, and the student-teacher-asshole ratio was nil. My mother often asked Chelsea how her day at school was. "Reeeally good" was Chelsea's general reply, which was proof-positive that nothing educational was happening. Chelsea continued to have minor flare-ups and meltdowns during her last two years at Happy High School, mostly mild bouts of teenage girl clinical insanity, but they were relatively benign compared to her much more turbulent early teen years.

The longer-term concern, though understated, was what the hell would happen with Chelsea when she was finished with Happy High School. The other five siblings had mysteriously found random professions—mechanical engineer, culinary chef, CPA, lawyer, and registered nurse—but somehow a profession didn't quite seem plausible or logical for Chelsea. She clearly didn't belong in college—or high school, for that matter. Neither my family nor I had any idea what would become of her. She was clearly entertaining to be with, but how was that going to translate into supporting herself, given her exasperating, volatile, and unpredictable daily behavior? Maybe she'd turn out fine, but she might just as easily spiral violently out of control. Because of her penchant for an off-the-charts lifestyle, I was impressed that she was even alive and had avoided a fatal accident, the mental ward, and spontaneous personal combustion.

After high school, she attended a semester and a half at the local county college, but everyone knew it was a charade, like putting a tomato in the microwave and expecting a nice glass of tomato juice to jump out after two minutes on high. After dropping out of college, she waited tables and drank her way around New Jersey for another year or two before getting bored. At that point, I used some frequent flyer miles and brought nineteen-year-old Chelsea to Los Angeles to visit our aunt, uncle, and nine cousins.

Before the return trip to the airport, I said, "Chelsea, let's go to LAX. We have to fly back to New Jersey."

She faked a polite "have a good flight" to me and stayed in Los Angeles for good. That was the beginning of Chelsea's brand-new foundation of fresh lies to be shared with a brand-new audience of unsuspecting Angelinos.

When I returned to New Jersey, my parents, in a rare act of parenting, asked, "Where's Chelsea, Glen?"

"Don't worry, Mom, Dad. I donated her to Los Angeles."

My brother Glen thinks that he is the funniest and smartest person in the family. He is funny, but I don't find him hilarious. They all had to put up with a lot of my chicanery and wild ways, and the truth is, they've all been rewarded tenfold for it.

—Chelsea

Exhibit A: The five of us in Anguilla this past Christmas. Shabbat shalom.

The following is an example of a typical birthday note Glen sends me each year. I'm convinced that he's convinced himself that he's a direct descendant of Socrates. The note's sentiment is nice, and imagine his surprise when I use one of these very same quotes when I give the commencement speech at Emory University this spring, the college he graduated from and I was denied entry to.

P.S.: For the record, I didn't get accepted into any college.

Holiday Inn®
Seoul

169-1, Dohwa-dong, Mapo-ku, Seoul, Korea Tel : (02)717-9441 Fax : (02)715-9441 Telex : Sgarden K24742 E-Mail : holidayi@aminet.co.kr

Let the black flower blossom as it may!

Nathaniel Hawthorne

Better be killed than frightened to death.

Robert Surtees

God's gifts put man's best dreams to shame.

Elizabeth Browning

It is only a rare man who has any tolerable knowledge of the character of even the women in his own family.

John Mill

The greater man, the greater courtesy. Alfred Tennyson

My heart is like a singing bird.

Christina Rossetti

That it will never come again ......
Is what makes life so sweet.

Emily Dickinson

It's a naive domestic Burgundy without any breeding, but I think you'll be amused by it's presumption.

James Thurber

Holiday Inn Seoul is owned and operated by Seoul Garden Hotel Co. Ltd., under license from Holiday Hospitality Corporation.
HGI-RD-002

258

Chapter Twelve

Standards and Practices

S&P is the abbreviation for Standards and Practices. This is the department of Comcast Entertainment that reminds us on a daily basis to bleep bad words we say on our show, and the department that attempts to rein us in when we've crossed the line, language- or taste-wise. Every day after we tape an episode of Chelsea Lately, we receive an e-mail from someone named Tom O'Brien outlining what needs to happen before the show airs on the East Coast.

It is hard for me to take seriously any department that specializes in monitoring me. Much like the gays in the South, the more the powers that be say no, the more I say, "Fuck off."

I have included what I consider to be the ten most amusing e-mail exchanges of this kind.

Sincerely,
Chesty

FROM: E! Entertainment Television
SENT: Monday, December 20, 2010, 1:50 PM
TO: Chelsea Lately Staff
SUBJECT: S&P Note for CL: jokes 5181

One S&P heads-up on today's script:

TOPIC #4 Vagina Steaming
   "Queef" will need to be bleeped, so you may want
to lose the joke.

Thanks

FROM: E! Entertainment Television

SENT: Monday, October 11, 2010, 4:02 PM

TO: Chelsea Lately Staff

SUBJECT: S&P notes for Chelsea Lately #5141, taped 10-11-10

Hi everyone,

Here are the S&P notes for today's show:

ROUNDTABLE

2:57: Welcome back. Let's talk about fingering. When specifically used in a sexual context, we can't go there. But a line like "This is as close as any girl is going to get to one of his fingers" is OK because that could mean a lot of things. In the lower 3rds, describing his new nail polish line as a "finger blast," it could be argued that you're talking about the bright color. (When "finger blast" is used in a sexual context, however, the phrase would have to be bleeped.) Well done. However, Chris' line about "having Justin Bieber's fingers in your daughter's vagina" paints too explicit a picture. Please lose the line. Thanks.

2:58: Please completely bleep "fucking" in "That wouldn't *fucking* help us."

3:00: Please completely bleep "shit" in "*Shit* that goes down there."

3:02: Please completely bleep "fuck" in *"Fuck* you."

3:09: Please completely bleep "shit" in "Oh *shit,* you're right."

TRACE ADKINS

3:16: Please completely bleep "fucking" in "He's a real *fucking* mess."

3:19: Please completely bleep "cock" in "Instead of saying *cock* . . ."

Thanks

FROM: E! Entertainment Television
SENT: Thursday, July 22, 2010, 4:17 PM
TO: Chelsea Lately Staff
SUBJECT: S&P notes for Chelsea Lately #5100, taped
7-22-10

Hi everyone,
Here are the S&P notes for today's show:
ROUNDTABLE
  3:11: Please completely bleep "shit" in "I'm too old
for this *shit*."
  3:13: Please completely bleep "fuck" in "He should
fuck Britney Spears."
  3:14: Please completely bleep "fucking" in "You
should *fucking* end it."
  3:15: Please completely bleep "shit" in "beat the *shit*
out of his fiancée."
  3:19: Please completely bleep "fucked" in "doubly
fucked."
  3:20: Please completely bleep "fuck" in "go *fuck*
herself."
  3:21: Please completely bleep "fucked" in "*fucked*
somebody's wife."

263

ARSENIO HALL

3:29: With regard to our previous discussions with Ted about using "shuttlecock" as a euphemism for penis ("shuttlecock" alone is OK but, when "cock" is paired with a word like "suck" as in "suck my shuttlecock," it's not, because of the sexual context), please lose Arsenio's *"suck her Cochran"* joke.

3:30: Please completely bleep "nigger" in "Put the *nigger* on the toilet."

3:30: Please completely bleep "shit" in "I don't give a *shit*."

Thanks

FROM: E! Entertainment Television

SENT: Tuesday, July 20, 2010, 4:21 PM

TO: Chelsea Lately Staff

SUBJECT: S&P notes for Chelsea Lately #5098, taped
           7-20-10

Hi everyone,

Here are the S&P notes for today's show:

ROUNDTABLE (SHOW #5098)

   3:09: Please completely bleep "shit" in Brad's "Aw *shit.*"

   3:11: Please completely bleep "Jesus" in Ben's "Aw *Jesus!*" (just as Chris comes on camera).

   3:14: Please lose Jo's retarded impersonation.

SUSAN SARANDON (SHOW #5098)

   3:27: Please completely bleep "shit" in "We'll ping-pong the *shit* out of Milwaukee."

CHICKEN CHARLIE (SHOW #5103)

   S&P approved.

Thanks

FROM: E! Entertainment Television

SENT: Thursday, November 18, 2010, 5:15 PM

TO: Chelsea Lately Staff

SUBJECT: S&P notes for Chelsea Lately #5165, taped
11-18-10

Hi everyone,
Here are the S&P notes for today's show:

ROUNDTABLE

Overall note: A lot of penis and vagina talk for our post-Thanksgiving show. Can we dial some of this back, particularly the "eating pussy" discussion in Act 2? Thanks.

4:27: Please completely bleep "fuck" in "Oh *fuck.*"

4:33: Please completely bleep "dick" in "Your Mom knows her way around a *dick.*"

4:35: Please completely bleep "pussy" in "And get some *pussy.*"

4:35: Please completely bleep "pussy" in "I want some of that *pussy.*"

4:36: Please completely bleep "pussy" in "oh, *pussy!*"

4:36: Please completely bleep the entire phrase "*eating pussy.*"

4:37: Please completely bleep "shit" in "You should hear the *shit* I say."

DONALD SCHULTZ

4:42: Please completely bleep "fucker" in "You little *fucker.*"

4:44: Please completely bleep "shit" in "Oh *shit.*"

4:45: Please completely bleep "hole" in "Look at that ass*hole.*"

Thanks

FROM: E! Entertainment Television
SENT: Monday, November 15, 2010, 4:51 PM
TO: Chelsea Lately Staff
SUBJECT: S&P notes for Chelsea Lately #5161, taped 11-15-10

Hi everyone,

Here are the S&P notes for today's show:

ROUNDTABLE (SHOW #5161)

3:42: Please completely bleep the entire phrase "jerking off" in Natasha's "You can't stop *jerking off* to porn."

3:45: No need for a fight on the "toilet babies" joke. It's incredibly tasteless, but it doesn't violate our standards. Besides, it's pretty funny.

3:47: Please completely bleep "fucked" in "Girls like that like to get *fucked.*"

MONICA POTTER (SHOW #5161)

4:02: Please completely bleep "fucking" and "holes" in "Those *fucking* ass*holes.*"

TREY SONGZ (SHOW #5162)

4:18: Please completely bleep "shit" in "Oh *shit.*"

4:21: Please completely bleep "shit" in "*Shit* can jump off." (Chelsea)

4:21: Please completely bleep "shit" in "*Shit* can jump off." (Trey)

Thanks

FROM: Tom O'Brien

SENT: Tuesday, July 21, 2009, 4:30 PM

TO: Chelsea Lately Staff

SUBJECT: S&P notes for Chelsea Lately #4093,
taped 7-21-09

Hi everyone,

Here are the S&P notes for today's taping:

ROUNDTABLE

3:11: Please completely bleep "shit" in "You guys
hear a ton of *shit*."

MARGARET CHO

- The "fags and fag hags" exchange. The word "fags"
  by itself is not acceptable in any circumstance,
  and every use of the word will need to be bleeped.
  Once before, we have allowed the term "fag hag"
  in an episode in a context that's very similar to the
  way Chelsea used it in today's roundtable discussion of the gay penguins. We're OK with that one
  use. But when Margaret repeatedly uses the term
  during the interview, it totally changes the tone of
  the program. We request that the term be bleeped
  throughout the interview or, ideally, the whole conversation be removed. Can we find another way to
  get into the "Project Runway" discussion?

- The description of the porn star's penis. The mention of his 9.2 inches is graphic but the quick mention is defendable. But Margaret crosses the line when she begins the detailed description and visuals of the volume of the penis and talks about her not being able to get it into her ass. It's just too graphic. Please lose.

Here are the line-by-line notes for the sequence:

3:23: Please completely bleep "shit" in "I think I'm a fat piece of *"shit."*

3:24: Please completely bleep "fags" and "fag hags" in "*fags* and *fag hags* fighting."

3:24: Please completely bleep "fags" and "fag hags" in "*fags* and *fag hags* together—there are going to be fights."

3:24: Please completely bleep "fag hag" in "Have you ever been a *fag hag?*"

3:24: Please completely bleep "fag hag" in "I am the biggest *fag hag* in the world."

3:24: Please completely bleep "fag hag" in "You are, you are a *fag hag.*"

3:24: Please completely bleep "fag hag" in "I am such a *fag hag.*"

3:24: Please completely bleep "fag hag" and "jerking off" in "I'm such a *fag hag,* now they're *jerking off* to me."

3:25: The 9.2 inch penis discussion. Please cut back per above.

3:25: Because it is used in a sexual context as a substitute for "penis," please completely bleep "*poppycock*."

3:26: We can get back into the interview around Chelsea's "putting things in your mouth" line.

Thanks

FROM: Chelsea Lately Staff

SENT: Wednesday, August 04, 2010, 1:09 PM

TO: E! Entertainment Television

SUBJECT: For approval, closing joke 5107

I tried to Tweet this photo this weekend and Twitter turned it down. Fortunately I have another outlet here at the E! Network. Suck on this Twitter.

Since my publisher is also preventing me from printing the photo due to its content, I will give you a full description. The photo is of three elderly men naked in bed together. Two are lying next to each other and French kissing; one man's hand is on the right breast of the recipient of the kiss, and the third gentleman is performing oral on the man who is getting his breast massaged while also getting a tongue in his mouth.

Obviously, this is what love is. Beautiful, natural, elderly love. The photo is called the Lemon Party. I highly recommend you Google it.

FROM: E! Entertainment Television
SENT: Wednesday, August 04, 2010, 1:49 PM
TO: Chelsea Lately Staff
SUBJECT: RE: For approval, closing joke 5107

Sorry, folks, but this photo isn't even remotely suitable for air. Please find another closing joke.

FROM: E! Entertainment Television

SENT: Monday, November 08, 2010, 2:26 PM

TO: Chelsea Lately Staff

SUBJECT: S&P Notes for CL: daily topics

Where to begin with Topic #2? And how do we keep this from going badly very quickly?

Since the topic is cunnilingus and the context is *only* sexual, all of our usual euphemisms (spicy tuna, dining at the Y, etc.) don't work here and will have to be bleeped or removed.

Just as we have to bleep both "suck" and "dick" in any topic about fellatio, in any jokes that contain the phrase "eat my pussy," both "eat" and "pussy" will have to be bleeped. This includes "eat my blank" (only indicates a sexual context) and the "Eat-vite" joke. (Again, there's no food context, so it only means cunnilingus.)

The "smell my finger" joke in this sexual context paints too graphic a picture. Please lose the joke.

In the past, Chelsea has usually sensed when the jokes are getting too explicit and tries to steer it away. That would be the best course of action today as well.

Thanks

No. Thank you, Comcast Entertainment.

—Chelsea

Chapter Thirteen

Raise the Woof

CHUNK

The extent to which Mom will lie has no limits. She lies to her friends, her coworkers, her family...even to her dog. I'm Chunk Handler and I'm Chelsea's dog. I am half-Asian and half-German shepherd. Please don't try to adjust the pages of this book. You read that correctly: I'm a dog. I have thoughts, dreams, and feelings all my own,

Me taking a dump.

and this is my story about the last time Mom pulled the dog fur over my eyes.

It was at our old place, sometime ago, and I was in the middle of another "home-school obedience lesson." Her then-boyfriend was constantly training me to "sit," "stay," and "heel." He always spoke real loud and slow, as if I'd just stepped off the short bus. So, as I said, he was trying to get me to do some dumb trick. I don't know. I wasn't really listening. I was just thinking, *How about I play dead, and you walk away for a long time?* Mom was watching this from across the kitchen, nursing a Belvedere and soda. She had pity in her eyes. I couldn't tell if it was pity for me or just self-pity. After a while of me pretending to be a dumb dog, her boyfriend got frustrated and huffed away. I couldn't believe this was going to be the rest of my life. I mean, it beats the dog pound, but it wasn't great either.

Once he was gone, Mom walked over to me, kneeled down, and said, "Don't worry, Chunk, I'm going to get us out of this mess." That was music to my ears. Finally, we were going to be alone.

A lot happened the next year. But the biggest development was that Mom and I moved out. All I ever wanted was a quiet place with no annoying people around. The large, modern home we moved into that summer was perfect—or so I thought.

"Lots of rooms," she'd asked for. I had hoped it was because she wanted to give me different areas to explore. But no, she wanted to fill those rooms with people. This was an "if you build it they will come" type of summer house. It had a giant pool, a diving board for her brother Roy, a big backyard, and a horse stable. Thank god those dumb horses moved out with the owners of the house. A horse is not my idea of a good time, and neither are the dumps they take. It was summer bliss but also summer hell, because I realized on the day we moved in that we were never going to be alone again.

It's not that I don't like people. I just think I'm better than most of them. There are a lot of idiots at Mom's office. And I have the reputation around there of being a little aloof and antisocial. These are some of the things I've heard them say about me behind my hairy back:

"That dog is an asshole," Johnny Kansas has repeatedly said, before I've even left a room.

Johnny, Mom calls you The Bird because your body is frail like a little girl's. Who's the asshole now?

"He's not my type of dog," said Chris Franjola one morning after I averted my eyes from his horse-like smile. The thought wasn't lost on me to store his ass in one of the stables at our new pad.

Chris, you don't have a type. Your only "type" is a girl dumb enough to text you naked pictures of herself. Thumbs up, my brother.

My first day at the office was kind of like my first day at the pound. Basically you have to find the weakest link and make him your bitch. I found a guy named Ryan Basford. He was the perfect man bitch. Just "goofy" enough to take

Chris Franjola

me on walks, feed me, and entertain me while Mom was too busy. He is also known to sit down when he urinates and to wipe his ass from back to front.

It was painful enough to spend most of my days with all the pedestrian people at Mom's work. But another little problem presented itself. His name was Jax, and he's a boxer. No, not a Mike Tyson–type boxer, because that would be cool. Jax is a boxer dog, and he pretty much sucks boxer balls.

Jax is a purebred, and purebreds are always such egomaniacs. They think they're so great looking, but usually they have a few screws loose upstairs due to inbreeding. He's also a real "man's dog," the type that's basically responsible for why dogs ever got the moniker "man's best friend" in the first place. Ironic that he belongs to a couple of lesbos.

Jax used to live in Dallas with the said lesbos, Shelly

Jax and me on one of the days Mom brought us to work.
Obviously, not ideal.

and Kelli. One day, about seven dog years ago, Mom and
I flew to Dallas with five of her friends after she ditched
her then-boyfriend. What happened between my mother
and Jax upon our arrival was one of the most horrific sights
I've ever seen. I can hardly think about it, let alone tell
the story. Johnny Kansas was sick enough to videotape Jax
forcing himself on my mom until she was on the ground,
and then humping her with his red rocket lipstick penis.
He was rubbing it all against her back as he licked her
entire face with his big tongue.

It was repulsive. It was like accidentally watching
a porn movie starring your mom and David Hasselhoff

having doggy-style sex on top of that stupid *Knight Rider* car, except there wasn't even a car. I didn't bother trying to protect my mother that day, because she was laughing, and I didn't want to look stupid. The main problem with my mother is that she laughs at everything, especially her own jokes.

As a big F-U to me, Jax and his lesbian moms ended up moving into our summer house. On top of that, Mom's brother Uncle Roy moved in with—get this—a fucking Jack Russell asshole who yapped from morning till night. Luckily, my mother got sick of that dog just as quickly as I did and had it transported on a pet airline to her sister Shoshanna in New Jersey. If I never see that dog again, it will be too soon.

On top of that, our quiet little abode soon became Grand Central Station for all of Mom's idiotic staff. It was like a new train came in every day with a fresh load of mumbling ignoramus passengers. It was the opposite of being alone. It was Moron Day every day. This was not turning out like I had planned. Or like how Mom had promised. Instead of dealing with one annoying person, I now had to deal with a whole array of them. I don't know if she realized it, but in getting me out of one mess she'd brought me into a much bigger mess altogether. On second thought, I bet she did realize it.

The constant barrage of irritation followed me to work as well. I mean, Jax literally followed me to Mom's office every day. Hanging out with that dog is like being at a sleepover with some kid you don't really like but your mom makes you hang out with him because she's friends with his mom. The hitch was that this sleepover never ended. Every night the dumb kid's like, "Hey, do you want to build a fort in the living room?" All I'm thinking is, *Yes, if you'll go inside it and stay there for a long time without me.*

The problem with Jax is that all the boneheads at Mom's office really like him. That's actually an understatement. They absolutely love that dog. And I get it. He's very "dog." He has a nice short coat that screams "I never have to get groomed but you can always see my muscles." He loves balls. I like saying that: "Jax loves balls." He runs up to everyone all happy-go-lucky. "Rub my belly!" this, "Scratch behind my ears!" that, "Hey! Let's play fetch!" He's always smiling, he's always happy. He's everything I'm not, and I'm forced to face that fact twenty-four hours a day.

It's really exhausting being around Jax. If my eyes could roll back any farther in my head in reaction to him, they would be staring at the front of my brain. I started hiding in the bathroom just to get away from everything. Like an old book in the public library, I often check myself out of the situation. Sometimes someone walks in, say, Elizabeth, Chelsea's assistant, and she'll be like, "Oh, poor Chunk, you got locked in the bathroom again . . . by accident. Here, let me bring you out."

No, Elizabeth, this is not an accident. I would rather sit on this cold tile floor in the bathroom, listening to the tinkle of girls going to the bathroom, than be subjected to everyone out there.

I'm just not part of that group, and I don't have to try to be. Mom loves me because I'm authentic to who I am, right? Not because I act like Jax, or like Johnny, or like Heather. I'm just different from all those people out there. I know dogs are supposed to be pack animals, but I feel more like a "pack of cigarettes" kind of animal. All I need is myself, my smokes, and that tornado of thoughts swirling around in my head. I don't really smoke. Because dogs can't actually smoke, you silly goose.

Which brings us to Mom's big Fourth of July pool party.

Los Angeles had been hit with a heat wave. I always thought a heat wave had something to do with a bunch of female dogs in heat waving at me. But I guess it just means that it gets hot as balls outside. (I don't have balls anymore, FYI.) So, due to this heat wave, Mom's lesbian stylist, Amy, had my entire body shaved to keep me cool, but they left the hair around my head and my neck all bushy. I looked like a stupid lion.

Hanging out at one of Mom's parties is like dropping acid and watching *Teletubbies*. All the usual suspects were in full form. Brad Wollack was under an umbrella applying SPF 200. He likes to brag about being a cancer survivor and that his sunscreen has to be specially ordered from Canada. Ben Gleib was busy running the Ping-Pong table, which is appropriately placed between the lesbian quarters and the horse stables. The camera guys were smoking pot somewhere. A topless security guard was playing badminton against himself. And Heather Long Boobs was walking around in a cocktail gown, which was way overdressed for a pool party. Heather's a real *C* word—a real cougar.

You get the idea. The party was a traveling circus full of carny-style freaks. You people wonder why I'm a little aloof and antisocial? Take a look at yourselves, you sickos. I'm not like you.

Mom had a new boyfriend at the time. I'll call him Salami, because his neck was so big it reminded me of a giant tube of salami. Anyway, Salami was some kind of "animal trainer," and I think he felt he needed to drive that point home by using me as his "animal trainee" all day. I tried telling him, "Look, you aren't the Dog Whisperer, and I'm not a wild lion from South Africa. So let's just try to have a normal relationship here and avoid each other."

Much to my dismay, Salami kept picking me up and walking around the party with me in his arms. It was humiliating. I'm not a lapdog. I'm a big dog, and big dogs don't get carried around in people's arms like that. To make matters worse, he carried me into the pool and started wading around the water with me still in his arms. Look, I'm a grown dog. If I want to go swimming, I'll do what normal dogs do and just jackknife off the diving board.

As I was wading around the pool with Salami, I noticed Jax barking at a bush. He is such a summer bummer. I can't believe Mom surrounded me with all these weirdos. If I had a cell phone, I would call my Chunk counterpart, Chocolate Chunk Sylvan, to come pick me up and drive me to the Jersey shore or somewhere else tropical. He has a nice big car, and he always drives Mom around when she's on tour.

Salami was done with our little synchronized swimming routine. Nobody seemed very impressed. He lifted me out of the pool and my wet body felt so naked without all my fur. So I ran inside to find my mom and complain about our new living situation.

That house is like a giant maze. I felt like a rat trying to find Cheese Whiz. I don't think I've even seen every room in the place yet. I cruised through one of the guest rooms and then into the bathroom. Oh shit, I didn't want to see that.

"Might want to knock," said some guy.

I had accidentally walked in on Geof, who was changing into a bathing suit.

"I don't have thumbs," I told him. "Makes it hard to knock." And I darted off.

Geof books all the shows for Mom's tour. I've got a few problems with this guy. First of all, he spells his name wrong. Second, he has more hair on his body than I do. Watching him apply sunscreen is like watching someone rub Ranch Dressing into a brown shag carpet. Doesn't that thick coat of body hair block the sun enough? And finally, since he's constantly taking Mom on the road, I barely get to see her anymore. In my opinion he overbooks her. I'm worried she's going to develop comedic fatigue stress syndrome disorder. I don't know if that's a real disease, but it sounds pretty serious. Mom's on tour a lot now. That's good for Geof, but it's bad for me. I really don't care about anybody's wellbeing other than mine and my mom's. Remember, people, the only person who's ever going to have your best interest in your life is yourself and your dog, if you have one. Unless your dog doesn't like you.

I passed through the kitchen, where Uncle Roy was cooking food for everyone. I think he likes cooking. I just don't think he likes cooking for all these thankless a-holes. Roy's head looks like a Macy's Thanksgiving Day Parade balloon, and his body is like those ropes holding the balloon to the ground. He never gives me table scraps. He's pretty much good for nothing.

Some dumb kid was munching out of a giant bowl of candy that Mom leaves out for them. It's like every generation of crazy is partying here today. These kids remind me of *Children of the Corn*, but today they're "Children of the Candy Corn" because they're stuffing fistfuls of it into their little saccharine-soaked bodies. I just hope they don't find any of the marijuana candy that's floating around here. On second thought, that would be really funny. I hope they find a lot of that marijuana candy that's floating around here. That'll teach them.

I passed by Chuy. He's the only person I really see eye to eye with. I stay out of his way; he stays out of mine. We have a common understanding. That's probably because we've both served time in the pound at one point in our lives.

Finally, after endless searching through this carnival un-funhouse I found my mom.

She was in the bedroom getting changed. Most people think it's so cool that she changes in front of me. First of all, she's my mom. And second of all, if you want to see her breasts all you have to do is get a job on her show. Everybody there gets to see those things at one point or another.

I figured this was my moment. It was my last chance to plead my case and to inject some sort of normalcy into her brain, so I said, "Mom, this situation is terrible. My summer is ruined. People think I'm an asshole and I don't even care, because all your friends and your brother, they're all freaks, and we can do better than them. It would be so much nicer with just you and me. So, what do you say? Take my paw, take my whole life, too. Let's get out of here, girl."

Of course, she couldn't understand a word I was saying because to her it all sounded like "pant pant pant pant pant pant pant." Someone should invent a device to translate dogs' thoughts. They'd make a killing.

So, Mom was like, "Oh hey, Chunk. Amy got you this really stupid cowboy hat and..." I was like, "Oh no you don't, girl," but it was too late. Mom strapped this ridiculous-looking spring break cowboy hat to my head and, against my will, sent me back out to the party. No surprise that everyone had a good hearty laugh at my expense.

Me at the fucking party.

I mean, all those whack jobs, and they were laughing at *me*? I couldn't believe it. Jax was still barking at a bush. The camera guys were getting drunker and more stoned. Roy was teaching my bitch, Ryan, how to dive into the pool. Chris Franjola was hitting on some girl young enough to be his granddaughter. And the topless security guard was still beating himself at badminton. Salami came over and lifted me up in his arms again.

"Ugh, will this ever stop?!" My head was starting to spin; the world was like a dreidel. I was hyperventilating, which, again, just looked like I was panting. I was ready to pass out. But then everything stopped, and my jaw dropped.

I caught my reflection in the pool and saw myself as the world saw me—as just another member of this motley crew. I realized that I had turned into one of them. I looked like a wet mutt/stupid lion/gay cowboy on spring break/half-Asian dog. I don't know if I'd always been such a misfit, or if I'd caught it, like the flu. All I knew was at that moment I truly was one of them.

Mom had said that she was going to get me out of that mess. And she had. But she'd brought me into a bigger mess. I guess her lie was that she never told me this was where I belonged. I belonged there because I was a mess, too. I'd always thought I was better than or different from all these people, but I guess I'm not. I'm like the pitcher on their dumbass softball team. I feel like such a dumb-dumb now for not seeing it all along.

You have to realize that if my mom picks on you, it's because she likes you. If she lies to you, it's because she loves you. All it means is that you're one of the lucky messes in her pack. And as I was looking around at all the oddballs and outcasts having a blast at her Fourth of July pool party, I realized that she hadn't rescued just me.

She'd rescued all of us.

———

I love you, too, Chunk. You're a real asshole, and I respect that. I'd also like to apologize for the bevy of men you've had to share our bed with. I have tried to be more selective in my thirties, but not every day is a home run. I do promise never to let another man pick you up and force you to swim in our pool. Thank you for your patience, and thank you for not being a racist during that one brief period.

—Chelsea

This is Michael Broussard, my book "agent," with his dog Dino (fucking mess), feeding alcohol to Chunk. As if I needed more proof, this made it clear that Chunk is my offspring.

Acknowledgments

Sarah Colonna, Sue Murphy, and Jeff Wild were also contributors to this book. They helped the people who have never taken part in a creative writing course or learned how to spell.

Me and Sue Murphy in the Bahamas.

Me and Sarah in Cabo.

Me and Jiffy at a Dodgers game in 2010.

Acknowledgments

A special thank you to my Borderline Amazing partner, Tom Brunelle, aka the man "behind" the scenes.

Me and Tom.